super-super cute crochet

super-super cute crochet

discover 35 fun and fluffy friends to crochet

Brigitte Read

CICO BOOKS
LONDON NEW YORK

Published in 2010 by CICO Books
an imprint of Ryland Peters & Small Ltd
519 Broadway, 5th Floor, New York, NY 10012

www.cicobooks.com

10 9 8 7 6 5 4 3 2 1

A CIP catalog record for this book is available from the Library
of Congress.

ISBN-13: 978 1 907030 25 3

Printed in China

Editor: Marie Clayton
Design: Luis Peral-Aranda
Style photography: Claire Richardson
Cutout photography: Paul Bricknall
Styling: Rob Merrett
Pattern checking: Jane Crowfoot and Luise Roberts

Contents

Introduction

I have been an avid crocheter for over 15 years, but when I saw my first amigurumi animal it really was love at first sight—I had to make one there and then! Amigurumi is the art of crocheting adorable stuffed animals, which started in Japan but has grown in popularity across the globe and I immediately became a fan. After I had successfully completed my first toy I was hooked. These were perfect for me; simple, fast, and so, so cute. I knew I had to make more! After a while spent getting used to how the patterns worked, I started making my own animals and decided to post them on a blog, Roman Sock (you can find it at littlegreen.typepad.com/romansock). It was one of the best decisions I've made and soon I was getting messages from other amigurumi fans who were admiring my designs and techniques, and wanting to get hold of my patterns. Well finally, here they are, I hope you like them!

Crochet is quite straightforward once you've mastered the basics. The patterns here are written to be accessible to beginners as well as more experienced crafters, so whatever your skill level, you will soon be making your own super-cute animals. If you're unsure of anything just refer to the techniques section at the back—it will tell you everything you need to know. Don't forget to try out the technique of brush crochet I developed. It's simple yet effective: all you need to do is brush the yarn quite roughly with a basic pet grooming brush—it really brings the toys to life.

I've had a lot of fun designing and making these 35 animals, and I hope you will too!

Farmyard friends

Pomeranian

Pomeranians are intelligent, very loyal, and their inquisitive nature means they are fun to be around. They need a loving owner and often bond closest to one person. Use this simple pattern to create your own perfect pom.

You will need...

- 25g DK/light worsted mohair/mohair mix, in lighter beige (MC) and darker orange (CC)
- E/4 (3.5mm) crochet hook
- Slicker brush
- 10mm black safety eyes, or two large beads
- Small scrap of brown or black dk yarn
- Yarn needle
- Around 8in. (20cm) of pipe cleaner
- Stuffing

abbreviations:

ch chain; inc increase; rep repeat; sc single crochet; sc2tog insert hook in st and draw up a loop. Insert hook in next st and draw up another loop. Yarn over, draw through all three loops on hook; ss slip stitch; st(s) stitch(es); tch turning chain

HEAD

When making the head, the idea is to make a ball shape, with one side beige and the other side orange.

Using MC, ch6, join with ss to make a ring.

Round 1: 2sc into each st. (12 sts)

Round 2: *2sc into next st, sc into each of foll 2 sts; rep from * three more times. (16 sts)

Round 3: *2sc into next st, sc into each of foll 3 sts; rep from * three more times. (20 sts)

Round 4: *2sc into next st, sc into each of foll 4 sts; rep from * three more times. (24 sts)

Rounds 5–6: Sc into each st.

Change to MC.

Round 7: Sc into each st.

Rounds 8–9: Sc2tog, sc in each st to end. (22 sts)

Brush head with slicker brush. Sew bead eyes or secure safety eyes onto head, on CC section.

Round 10: Sc into each of the foll 2 sts, *sc2tog, sc into each of foll 3 sts; rep from * three more times. (18 sts)

Round 11: Sc into each of the foll 2 sts, *sc2tog, sc into each of foll 2 sts; rep from * three more times. (14 sts)

Round 11: Sc into each of the foll 2 sts, *sc2tog, sc into next st; rep from * three more times. (10 sts)

Fasten off.

NOSE

Using CC, ch8 join with ss to make a ring.

Round 1: Sc in each st.

Round 2: 2sc into next st, sc into each st to the end. (9 sts)

Rounds 3–4: Sc in each st.

Fasten off.

BODY

Using CC, ch7.

Round 1: Sc in each st.

Round 2: 2sc in each st. (14 sts)

Round 3: *2sc into next st, sc into next st; rep from * six more times. (21 sts)

Round 4: *Sc into each of the foll 6 sts, 2sc into next st; rep from * twice more. (24 sts)

Round 5: Sc in each st, 1tch. (24 sts).

Turn work and cont to work in rows.

Rows 1–8: Sc into each of next 8 sts, 1tch. (8 sts)

Fasten off.

This should create a rectangle coming off from the circle.

With the CC-rectangle to the right, join MC into the next st on round 5, and cont to work in rows.

Rows 1–9: Sc into each of next 16 sts, 1tch. (16 sts)

This creates a circular base with two rectangular blocks of color, which will be sewn together later.

Using MC.

Next round: Sc in each st across the top of the CC-rectangle and then the MC-rectangle to complete the round. (24 sts)

Next round: *Sc into each of the foll 6 sts, sc2tog; rep from * twice more. (21 sts)

Next round: *Sc into next st, sc2tog; rep from * six times more. (14 sts)

Next round: Sc2tog seven times. (7 sts)

Fasten off.

Sew the two splits together.

FRONT LEGS (MAKE 2)

Work around a pipe cleaner, or insert pipe cleaner afterwards.

Using MC, ch7 join with ss to make a ring.

Rounds 1–9: Sc into each st. (6 sts)

Fasten off.

BACK LEGS (MAKE 2)

Work around a pipe cleaner, or insert pipe cleaner afterwards.

Using MC, ch7 join with ss to make a ring.

Rounds 1–4: Sc into each st (7 sts)

Round 5: Sc into the next st, *sc2tog, sc into foll st; rep from * once more. (5 sts)

Rounds 6–10: Sc into each st. (5 sts)

Fasten off.

EARS (MAKE 2)

Using CC, ch6 plus one tch.

Work in rows, do not use tch so each row reduces by one st.

Row 1: Sc into the 2nd ch from the hook, sc into each ch to the end, turn. (5 sts)

Row 2: Sc into each st, turn. (4 sts)

Row 3: Sc into each st, turn. (3 sts)

Row 4: Sc into each st, turn. (2 sts)

Row 5: Sc into each st, turn. (1 st)

Fasten off.

TAIL

Using MC, ch9 plus 1tch.

Next row: Sc into the 2nd ch from the hook, sc into each st to the end. (8 sts)

Fasten off.

FINISHING

Stuff body. Brush out the nose and stitch onto head. Using brown yarn and yarn needle, embroider a nose onto the end of snout, around the same size as eyes. Trim hair to make the pom face. Tidy the legs up by trimming excess pipe cleaner, closing the ends and weaving in any loose ends. Brush each piece with the slicker brush until fluffy—you will have to brush from many different angles to get the best effect. Stitch the ears onto the head, then the head onto the body, using the photograph on page 10 to get the right look. Stitch the legs onto the body, and shape the body appropriately. Stitch on the tail, which should curl up onto the back. Trim the fur on the legs and body.

FINISHED SIZE: approx 6in. (15cm) high

Bunny rabbit

This rabbit has a face so cute that it's hard for even the most ardent gardener not to forgive his forays into the vegetable patch in search of food. They would have to be pretty fast, too, in order to catch him, as this little chap can move at quite a pace. He uses his oversized ears to detect predators, and when he hears one coming he'll turn tail and be back safely underground in seconds.

FRONT HEAD

Work in a continuous spiral.

Using MC, make a yarn ring, work 6sc into the ring.

Round 1: 2sc into each st to end of round. (12 sts)

Round 2: *1sc into next st, 2sc into foll st; rep from * to end of round. (15sts)

Round 3: *1sc into next 2 sts, 2sc into foll st; rep from * to end of round. (20 sts)

Round 4: *1sc into next 3 sts, 2sc into foll st; rep from * to end of round. (25 sts)

Round 5: *1sc into next 4 sts, 2sc into foll st; rep from * to end of round. (30 sts)

Round 6: *1sc into next 5 sts, 2sc into foll st; rep from * to end of round. (35 sts)

Rounds 7–10: 1sc into each st to end of round. Fasten off.

BACK HEAD

Using MC, ch11.

Row 1: Work sc into each st to end of chain. (10 sts)

Rows 2–8: 1sc into each st to end of round. Fasten off.

BODY TOP

Work in a continuous spiral.

Using MC, make a yarn ring, work 6sc into the ring.

Round 1: 2sc into each st to end of round. (12 sts)

Round 2: *1sc into next st, 2sc into foll st; rep from * to end of round. (18 sts)

Round 3: *1sc into next 2 sts, 2sc into foll st; rep from * to end of round. (24 sts)

Round 4: *1sc into next 3 sts, 2sc into foll st; rep from * to end of round. (30 sts)

Round 5: *1sc into next 4 sts, 2sc into foll st; rep from * to end of round. (36 sts)

Round 6: *1sc into next 5 sts, 2sc into foll st; rep from * to end of round. (42 sts)

Round 7: *1sc into next 6 sts, 2sc into foll st; rep from * to end of round. (46 sts)

Rounds 8–12: 1sc into each st to end of round. Fasten off.

BODY BASE

Using A, work as for body to end of round 7.

Round 8: 1sc into each st to end of round. Fasten off.

FRONT LEGS (MAKE 2)

Using MC, ch6, join with ss to make a ring. Work 6sc into center of ring.

Round 1: 2sc into each st to end of round. (12 sts)

Round 2: *1sc into next st, 2sc into foll st; rep from * to end of round. (15 sts)

You will need...

- 50g DK/light worsted yarn in Gray (MC)
- 10g same in White (A)
- 10g same in Pink (B)
- E/4 (3.5 mm) crochet hook
- Stuffing
- Pair of 7.5mm black safety eyes
- Yarn needle

abbreviations:

ch chain; **foll** following; **inc** increase; **rep** repeat; **sc** single crochet; **sc2tog** insert hook in st and draw up a loop. Insert hook in next st and draw up another loop. Yarn over, draw through all three loops on hook; **ss** slip stitch; **st(s)** stitch(es)

Rounds 3–4: 1sc into each st to end of round.
Fasten off.

BACK LEGS (MAKE 2)
Using MC, ch6.
Row 1: 1sc into each st to end of ch. (5 sts)
Rows 2–8: 1sc into each st to end of round.
Leave final stitch loop on hook. Work 18sc
around outside edge of rectangle.
Fasten off.

PAWS (MAKE 4)
Using A, ch6, join with ss to make a ring. Work
6sc into center of ring.
Round 1: 2sc into each st to end of round.
(12 sts)
Round 2: *1sc into next st, 2sc into foll st; rep
from * to end of round. (15 sts)

EARS (MAKE 2)
Using MC, ch6.
Row 1: 1sc into each st to end of ch. (5 sts)
Rows 2–16: 1sc into each st to end of round.
Row 17: Sc2tog, 1sc into foll st, sc2tog. (3 sts)
Fasten off.
With RS facing, rejoin yarn and work 34sc
around outside edge of ear.
Fasten off.

FINISHING
Using A, embroider V shapes either side of the
head to represent whites of eyes. Secure safety
eyes to head through center of embroidery.
Stuff head. Sew back head to front head, leaving
seam open at top of head. Insert ears into the
gap and complete the seam sewing ears into
place as you sew. Using B, embroider nose at
front of head.
Stuff body top and sew to body base. Stuff
each leg and sew paws to underside of legs.
Sew in place on the body using the photograph
on page 12 as a guide.

TAIL
Using A, ch2.
Wrap yarn round hook 7 times, insert hook
into first ch, wrap yarn round hook and draw
through all loops, 1ch.
Fasten off.
Sew in place at back end of body.

FINISHED SIZE: approx 5in. (12.5cm) long

Kitten

Kittens are naturally curious and playful, and will always be on the look out for new people and toys to play with. This fluffy tabby has managed to get into the knitting basket—he's got a thing for wool.

You will need...

- 25g DK/light worsted fluffy yarn (such as Sirdar Blur) in Gray
- E/4 (3.5mm) crochet hook
- Stuffing
- 2 small black beads, or pair of safety eyes
- Bead for nose or a small amount of DK/light worsted yarn in Pink
- Black embroidery thread
- Yarn needle

abbreviations:

ch chain; foll following; inc increase; rep repeat; sc single crochet; sc2tog insert hook in st and draw up a loop. Insert hook in next st and draw up another loop. Yarn over, draw through all three loops on hook; ss slip stitch; st(s) stitch(es); tch turning chain

BODY

Work in a continuous spiral.

Make a yarn ring, work 6sc into the ring.

Round 1: 2sc in each st to end of round. (12 sts)

Round 2: *1sc into next 3 sts, 2sc into foll st; rep from * twice more. (15 sts)

Round 3: *1sc into next 2 sts, 2sc into foll st; rep from * four times more. (20 sts)

Round 4: *1sc into next 3 sts, 2sc into foll st; rep from * four times more. (25 sts)

Round 5: *1sc into next 4 sts, 2sc into foll st; rep from * four times more. (30 sts)

Round 6: *1sc into next 5 sts, 2sc into foll st; rep from * four times more. (35 sts)

Round 7: *1sc into next 6 sts, 2sc into foll st; rep from * four times more. (40 sts)

Round 8: *1sc into next 7 sts, 2sc into foll st;** rep from * four times more.** (45 sts)

Rounds 9–27: Work in sc throughout. Fasten off.

HEAD (MAKE 2)

Work in a continuous spiral.

Make a yarn ring, work 6sc into the ring.

Work as for body to **.

Round 9: *1sc into next 8 sts, 2sc into foll st; rep from * four times more. (50 sts) Fasten off.

LEGS (MAKE 4)

Work in a continuous spiral.

Make a yarn ring, work 8sc into the ring.

Rounds 1–10: Work in sc throughout. Fasten off.

TAIL

Work in a continuous spiral.

Make a yarn ring, work 6sc into the ring.

Rounds 1–15: Work in sc throughout. Fasten off.

EARS (MAKE 2)

Ch5. Work without tch to decrease on each row.

Row 1: 1sc into each st. (5 sts)
Row 2: 1sc into each st. (4 sts)
Row 3: 1sc into each st. (3 sts)
Row 4: 1sc into each st. (2 sts)
Row 5: 1sc into each st. (1 st)
Fasten off.

FINISHING

Sew bead eyes or attach safety eyes onto head. Add nose bead, or embroider a nose using Pink yarn. Sew together the head leaving a small gap. Stuff lightly. Sew remaining seam, attach the ears. Stuff the body lightly and sew together the top seam. Using the photograph on page 17 as a guide, sew the head, legs and tail onto the body. Embroider claws and a mouth with black embroidery thread.

FINISHED SIZE: approx 7in. (17.5cm) long

Percy pig

If you want this little piggy to stay in the pink you will need to keep an eye on him. Like most pigs, Percy adores mud, and at the first chance he gets he will make a dash for it. You can make up for a lack of mud with lots of cuddles and games. But beware; if he spots a nice muddy puddle from the corner of his eye, chances are you are in for a thorough splashing.

HEAD AND BODY
The body is made in two pieces.
Work in a continuous spiral.
Ch6, join with ss to make a ring.
Round 1: Working into the front of the st, work 1dc into each st to end of round. (6 sts)
Round 2: 1sc into each st to end. (6 sts)
Round 3: 1sc into next 2 sts, place a marker in both sts, work 2sc in each st to marker. (10 sts)
Round 4: 1sc into next 2 sts, place a marker in both sts, *1sc in next st, 2dc in foll st; rep from * to marker. (14 sts)
Round 5: 1sc into next 2 sts, place a marker in both sts, *1sc in next 2 sts, 2dc in foll st; rep from * to marker. (18 sts)
Rounds 6–14: Work without inc.
Fasten off.

BODY REAR
Work in a continuous spiral.
Make a yarn ring, work 6sc into the ring.
Round 1: 2sc in each st to end of round. (12 sts)
Round 2: *1sc into next st, 2sc in foll st; rep from * to end. (18 sts)
Round 3: Work in sc throughout.
Fasten off, leaving a long end.

LEGS (MAKE 4)
Work in a continuous spiral.
Make a yarn ring, work 6sc into the ring.
Rounds 1–4: Work in sc throughout.
Fasten off.

EARS (MAKE 2)
Ch4 and secure on head with slip stitch.
Fasten off.

FINISHING
Sew bead eyes or safety eyes onto head. Stuff head, body and rear and sew together. Sew legs onto underside of body. Sew ears on either side of head. Using yarn end on rear, create a chain tail.

FINISHED SIZE: approx 2½in. (6cm) long

You will need...

- 25g DK/light worsted alpaca in Pink
- E/4 (3.5mm) crochet hook
- Pair of safety eyes or 5mm beads
- Stuffing
- Yarn needle

abbreviations
ch chain; **dc** double crochet; **cont** continue; **foll** following; **inc** increase; **rep** repeat; **sc** single crochet; **ss** slip stitch; **st(s)** stitch(es)

Siberian hamster

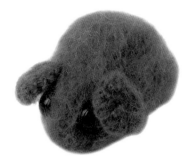

Siberian hamsters are more friendly towards humans than other varieties. These tiny crocheted versions, with their fluffy long hair, take no time at all to make and look adorable when finished. Why not make a few?

You will need...

- 25g DK/light worsted fluffy yarn (such as Sirdar Blur) in Brown
- E/4 (3.5mm) crochet hook
- Pair of 5mm safety eyes or two small black beads
- Yarn needle

abbreviations:

ch chain; **foll** following; **inc** increase; **rep** repeat; **sc** single crochet; **sc2tog** insert hook in st and draw up a loop. Insert hook in next st and draw up another loop. Yarn over, draw through all three loops on hook; **ss** slip stitch; **st(s)** stitch(es)

HEAD AND BODY
The body is made in two pieces.
Work in a continuous spiral.
Make a yarn ring, work 6sc into the ring.
Round 1: 1sc in each st to end of round. (6 sts)
Rounds 2–3: Work without inc.
Round 4: *2sc in next st, 1sc in foll st; rep from * twice more. (9 sts)
Round 5: *2sc in next st, 1sc in foll 2 sts; rep from * twice more. (12 sts)
Round 6: *2sc in next st, 1sc in foll st; rep from * five times more. (18 sts)
Round 7: Work without inc.
Round 8: *2sc in next st, 1sc in foll 2 sts; rep from * five times more. (24 sts)
Round 9: *2sc in next st, 1sc in foll 3 sts; rep from * five times more. (30 sts)
Rounds 10–14: Work without inc.
Fasten off.

BODY BASE
Work in a continuous spiral.
Make a yarn ring, work 6sc into the ring.
Round 1: 1sc in each st to end of round. (6 sts)
Round 2: 2sc in each st to end of round. (12 sts)
Round 3: *2sc in next st, 1sc in foll st; rep from * five times more. (18 sts)
Round 4: *2sc in next st, 1sc in foll 2 sts; rep from * five times more. (24 sts)
Round 5: *2sc in next st, 1sc in foll 3 sts; rep from * five times more. (30 sts)
Fasten off.

EAR (MAKE 2)
Ch6, join with ss to make a ring.
Round 1: *2sc into next st, sc into foll st; rep from * twice more. (9 sts)
Round 2: *2sc into next st, sc into each of foll 2 sts; rep from * twice more. (12 sts)
Round 3: *1sc into each of next 3 sts, 2sc into foll st; rep from * twice more. (15 sts)
Fasten off.

TAIL
Join yarn into a st at base of the rear, work 10ch, ss into st at base of ch.
Fasten off.

FINISHING
Sew bead eyes or safety eyes onto head, and attach ears. Stuff body and rear body and sew together.

FINISHED SIZE: approx 3in. (7.5cm) long

Puppy

There's nothing a puppy loves more than a bowl full of bone-shaped biscuits. Since they are growing animals, their appetites are insatiable, and if left alone for even a second they will be on the hunt for more munchies. Dogs are intelligent animals and like a challenge, so be careful where you store your treats, because a puppy like this one will try his hardest to find a way to get to them and will probably succeed!

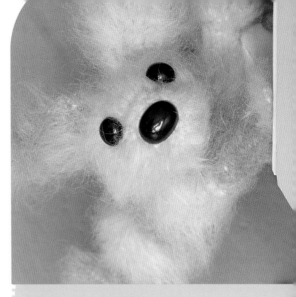

BODY
Ch6, join with ss to make a ring.
Round 1: *2sc into next st, 1sc; rep from * twice more. (9 sts)
Round 2: *2sc into next st, 1sc into foll 2 sts; rep from * twice more. (12 sts)
Round 3: *1sc into next 3 sts, 2sc into foll st; rep from * twice more. (15 sts)
Round 4: *1sc into next 2 sts, 2sc into foll st; rep from * four times more. (20 sts)
Round 5: *1sc into next 3 sts, 2sc into foll st; rep from * four times more. (25 sts)
Round 6: *1sc into next 4 sts, 2sc into foll st; rep from * four times more. (30 sts)
Round 7: *1sc into next 5 sts, 2sc into foll st; rep from * four times more. (35 sts)
Round 8: *1sc into next 6 sts, 2sc into foll st; rep from * four times more. (40 sts)
Rounds 9–31: Work without inc.
Round 32: *1sc into next 6 sts, sc2tog; rep from * four times more. (35 sts)
Round 33: *1sc into next 5 sts, sc2tog; rep from * four times more. (30 sts)
Round 34: *1sc into next 4 sts, sc2tog; rep from * four times more. (25 sts)
Round 35: *1sc into next 3 sts, sc2tog; rep from * four times more. (20 sts)
Round 36: *1sc into next 2 sts, sc2tog; rep from * four times more. (15 sts)

Stuff body.
Round 37: *1sc into next 3 sts, sc2tog; rep from * twice more. (12 sts)
Round 38: *Sc2tog, 1sc into foll 2 sts; rep from * twice more. (9 sts)
Round 39: *Sc2tog, 1sc; rep from * twice more. (6 sts)
Fasten off.

HEAD
Ch6, join with ss to make a ring.
Round 1: *2sc into next st, 1sc; rep from * twice more. (9 sts)
Round 2: *2sc into next st, 1sc into foll 2 sts; rep from * twice more. (12 sts)
Round 3: *1sc into next 3 sts, 2sc into foll st; rep from * twice more. (15 sts)
Round 4: *1sc into next 2 sts, 2sc into foll st; rep from * four times more. (20 sts)
Round 5: *1sc into next 3 sts, 2sc into foll st; rep from * four times more. (25 sts)
Round 6: *1sc into next 4 sts, 2sc into foll st; rep from * four times more. (30 sts)
Round 7: *1sc into next 5 sts, 2sc into foll st; rep from * four times more. (35 sts)
Rounds 8–10: Work without inc.
Round 11: *1sc into next 5 sts, sc2tog; rep from * four times more. (30 sts)

You will need...

- 50g DK/light worsted fluffy yarn in Beige
- E/4 (3.5mm) crochet hook
- Pair of 12mm black safety eyes
- Stuffing
- Slicker brush
- 15mm wide oval black safety nose
- Yarn needle

abbreviations:

ch chain; **dc** double crochet; **foll** following; **inc** increase; **rep** repeat; **sc** single crochet; **sc2tog** insert hook in st and draw up a loop. Insert hook in next st and draw up another loop. Yarn over, draw through all three loops on hook; **ss** slip stitch; **st(s)** stitch(es)

Round 12: *1sc into next 4 sts, sc2tog; rep from * four times more. (25 sts)

Round 13: *1sc into next 3 sts, sc2tog; rep from * four times more. (20 sts)

Round 14: *1sc into next 2 sts, sc2tog; rep from * four times more. (15 sts)

Secure safety eyes and nose, stuff head.

Round 15: *1sc into next 3 sts, sc2tog; rep from * twice more. (12 sts)

Round 16: *Sc2tog, 1sc into foll 2 sts; rep from * twice more. (9 sts)

Round 17: *Sc2tog, 1sc; rep from * twice more. (6 sts)

Fasten off.

SNOUT

Ch6, join with ss to make a ring.

Round 1: *2sc into next st, 1sc; rep from * twice more. (9 sts)

Round 2: *2sc into next st, 1sc into foll 2 sts; rep from * twice more. (12 sts)

Round 3: *1sc into next 3 sts, 2sc into foll st; rep from * twice more. (15 sts)

Round 4: *1sc into next 2 sts, 2sc into foll st; rep from * four times more. (20 sts)

Rounds 5–6: Work without inc.

Fasten off.

LEGS AND FEET (MAKE 4)

Ch6, join with ss to make a ring.

Round 1: *2sc into next st, 1sc; rep from * twice more. (9 sts)

Round 2: *2sc into next st, 1sc into foll 2 sts; rep from * twice more. (12 sts)

Rounds 3–10: Work without inc.

Round 11: *1sc into next st, 4dc into foll st, skip 1 st 1sc into the foll st: rep from, * twice more. Fasten off.

EARS (MAKE 2)

Ch6 plus one tch.

Row 1: Sc into the 2nd ch from the hook, sc each ch to the end, 1tch. (6 sts)

Rows 2–8: Sc into each st, 1tch. (6 sts)

Fasten off.

TAIL

Rejoin yarn to the back of the body, ch10, ss into the the 2nd ch from the hook, ss into each ch to the end.

Fasten off.

FINISHING

Brush all the pieces thoroughly with the slicker brush. Sew ears and snout onto head. Sew head and legs onto body.

FINISHED SIZE: approx 6in. (15cm) long

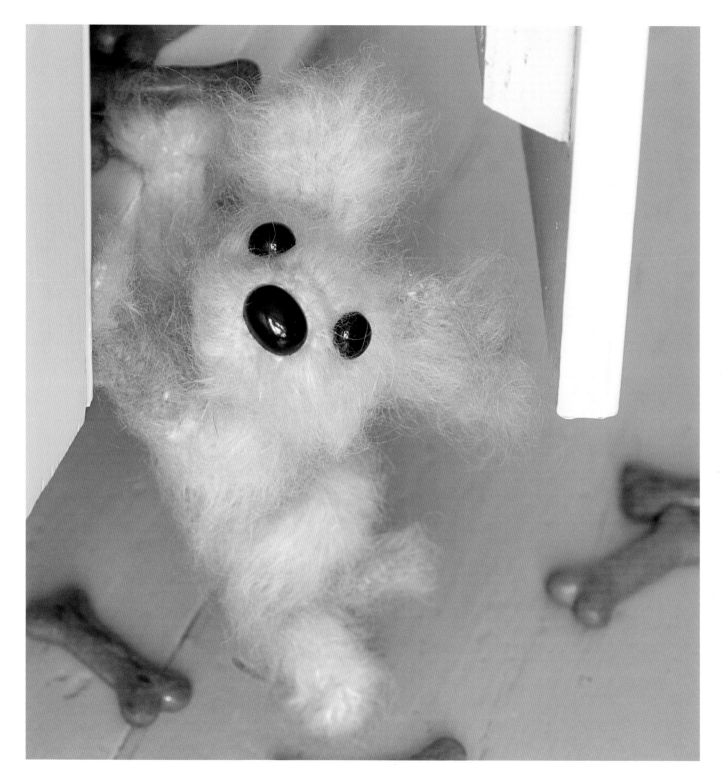

Cat

In some cultures black cats get a negative press since they are often associated with bad luck. This little guy prefers the idea that if a black cat arrives on your doorstep it's a sign of prosperity. Look out for him coming to a home near you soon.

You will need...

- 20g DK/light worsted yarn in Black MC
- 10g same in White CC
- E/4 (3.5mm) crochet hook
- Stuffing
- Pair of 15mm safety cat eyes
- Yarn needle

abbreviations:

ch chain; foll following; inc increase; rep repeat; sc single crochet; sc2tog insert hook in st and draw up a loop. Insert hook in next st and draw up another loop. Yarn over, draw through all three loops on hook; ss slip stitch; st(s) stitch(es); tch turning chain

BODY

Using MC, ch6, join with ss to make a ring.
Round 1: *2sc into next st, sc into foll st; rep from * twice more. (9 sts)
Round 2: *2sc into next st, sc into each of foll 2 sts; rep from * twice more. (12 sts)
Round 3: *1sc into each of next 3 sts, 2sc into foll st; rep from * twice more. (15 sts)
Round 4: *1sc into each of next 2 sts, 2sc into foll st; rep from * four times more. (20 sts)
Round 5: *1sc into each of next 3 sts, 2sc into foll st; rep from * four times more. (25 sts)
Round 6: *1sc into each of next 4 sts, 2sc into foll st; rep from * four times more. (30 sts)
Round 7: *1sc into each of next 5 sts, 2sc into foll st; rep from * four times more. (35 sts)
Round 8: *1sc into each of next 6 sts, 2sc into foll st; rep from * four times more. (40 sts)
Rounds 9–31: Work without inc.
Round 32: *1sc into each of next 6 sts, sc2tog; rep from * four times more. (35 sts)
Round 33: *1sc into each of next 5 sts, sc2tog; rep from * four times more. (30 sts)
Round 34: *1sc into each of next 4 sts, sc2tog; rep from * four times more. (25 sts)
Round 35: *1sc into each of next 3 sts, sc2tog; rep from * four times more. (20 sts)
Round 36: *1sc into each of next 2 sts, sc2tog; rep from * four times more. (15 sts)
Stuff body.
Round 37: *1sc into each of next 3 sts, sc2tog; rep from * twice more. (12 sts)
Round 38: *Sc2tog, sc into each of foll 2 sts; rep from * twice more. (9 sts)
Round 39: *Sc2tog, sc into foll st; rep from * twice more. (6 sts).
Fasten off.

HEAD

Using MC, ch6, join with ss to make a ring.
Round 1: *2sc into next st, sc into foll st; rep from * twice more. (9 sts)
Round 2: *2sc into next st, sc into each of foll 2 sts; rep from * twice more. (12 sts)
Round 3: *1sc into each of next 3 sts, 2sc into foll st; rep from * twice more. (15 sts)
Round 4: *1sc into each of next 2 sts, 2sc into foll st; rep from * four times more. (20 sts)
Round 5: *1sc into each of next 3 sts, 2sc into foll st; rep from * four times more. (25 sts)
Round 6: *1sc into each of next 4 sts, 2sc into foll st; rep from * four times more. (30 sts)
Round 7: *1sc into each of next 5 sts, 2sc into foll st; rep from * four times more. (35 sts)
Round 8: *1sc into each of next 6 sts, 2sc into foll st; four times more. (40 sts)
Rounds 9–10: Work without inc.
Round 11: *1sc into each of next 6 sts, sc2tog; rep from * four times more. (35 sts)
Round 12: *1sc into each of next 5 sts, sc2tog; rep from * four times more. (30 sts)
Round 13: *1sc into each of next 4 sts, sc2tog; rep from * four times more. (25 sts)
Round 14: *1sc into each of next 3 sts, sc2tog; rep from * four times more. (20 sts)
Round 15: *1sc into each of next 2 sts, sc2tog; rep from * four times more. (15 sts)
Secure safety eyes and stuff head.

Round 16: *1sc into each of next 3 sts, sc2tog; rep from * twice more. (12 sts)

Round 17: *Sc2tog, sc into each of foll 2 sts; rep from * twice more. (9 sts)

Round 18: *Sc2tog, sc into foll st; rep from * twice more. (6 sts). Fasten off.

SNOUT

Using CC, ch6, join with ss to make a ring.

Round 1: *2sc into next st, sc into foll st; rep from * twice more. (9 sts)

Round 2: *2sc into next st, sc into each of foll 2 sts; rep from * twice more. (12 sts)

Round 3: *1sc into each of next 3 sts, 2sc into foll st; rep from * twice more. (15 sts)

Round 4: *1sc into each of next 2 sts, 2sc into foll st; rep from * four times more. (20 sts)

Round 5: *1sc into each of next 3 sts, 2sc into foll st; rep from * four times more. (25 sts) Fasten off.

FEET (MAKE 4)

Using CC, ch6, join with ss to make a ring.

Round 1: *2sc into next st, sc into foll st; rep from * twice more. (9 sts)

Round 2: *2sc into next st, sc into each of foll 2 sts; rep from * twice more. (12 sts)

Round 3: *1sc into each of next 3 sts, 2sc into foll st; rep from * twice more. (15 sts) Fasten off.

FINISHING

Sew head, snout, and feet to body.

EARS (MAKE 2)

Rejoin yarn and sc 8 sts across one side of head, using the photograph as a guide, then decrease naturally on each row by not using a tch. Repeat on the other side for the second ear. Work one row of sc around the edge of each ear to neaten.

TAIL

Rejoin yarn into the rear of the body, ch 10, then fasten off.

FINISHED SIZE: approx 8in. (20cm) long

Cow

The first cow arrived in the U.S. in 1611 and now there are nearly 100 million of them! The majority are black and white Holsteins, like this crocheted one.

BODY AND HEAD
The body is made in two pieces.
Using MC, ch19.
Row 1: 1sc into each ch, 1tch, turn. (18 sts)
Rows 2–14: 1sc into each st, 1tch, turn. (18 sts)
Row 15: 1sc into each st, 1ch. Do not turn. (18 sts)
Next Row: Work 15sc along left side edge of rectangle, 18sc along foundation chain, 15sc along right side edge and 18sc along top edge, ss into first sc, 1ch. Do not turn. (66 sts)
Work 12 rows as set.
Fasten off.

BODY BASE
Using MC, ch19.
Row 1: 1sc into each ch, 1tch, turn. (18 sts)
Rows 2–14: 1sc into each st, 1tch, turn. (18 sts)
Row 15: 1sc into each st, 1ch. (18 sts)
Fasten off.

NOSE
Using B, ch10.
Row 1: 1sc into each st, 1tch, turn. (9 sts)
Rows 2–4: 1sc into each st, 1tch, turn. (9 sts)
Row 5: 1sc into each st, 1ch. Do not turn. (9 sts)
Next Row: Work 5sc along left side edge of rectangle, 9sc along foundation chain, 5sc along right side edge and 9sc along top edge, ss into first sc, 1tch. (28 sts)
Work 4 rows as set.
Fasten off.

FINISHING
Turn the body piece so that the wrong side is facing (this is now the right side).
Using A and long oversewn stitches, embroider some patches onto the body, using the photograph on page 28 as a guide.
Stuff the nose and sew in place at one end of the body piece. Secure safety eyes in place above the nose. Stuff body and sew body base in place.

TAIL
Using A, ch6 and fasten off. Sew onto end of body.

EARS (MAKE 2)
Using MC, ch6 and fasten off. Hold each ear chain in a loop and sew into place above eyes.

FINISHED SIZE: approx 6in. (15cm) long

You will need...

- 50g Chunky yarn in White (MC)
- 25g same in Black (A)
- 25g same in Pink (B)
- E/4 (3.5mm) crochet hook
- Stuffing
- Pair of 15mm safety eyes
- Yarn needle

abbreviations:

ch chain; **inc** increase; **rep** repeat; **sc** single crochet; **sc2tog** insert hook in st and draw up a loop. Insert hook in next st and draw up another loop. Yarn over, draw through all three loops on hook; **ss** slip stitch; **st(s)** stitch(es); **tch** turning chain

The life aquatic

Polar bear

The fur of a polar bear appears white but is actually transparent, unlike the white yarn used to give these bears a fluffy finish.

HEAD AND BODY

The body is made in two pieces. Work in a continuous spiral. Using MC, make a yarn ring, work 6sc into the ring.

Rounds 1–2: Work without inc. (6 sts)

Round 3: *2sc into next st, 1sc; rep from * twice more. (9 sts)

Round 4: *2sc into next st, 1sc into foll 3 sts; rep from * twice more. (12 sts)

Round 5: *1sc into next 3 sts, 2sc into foll st; rep from * twice more. (15 sts)

Round 6: *1sc into next 2 sts, 2sc into foll st; rep from * four times more. (20 sts)

Round 7: *1sc into next 3 sts, 2sc into foll st; rep from * four times more. (25 sts)

Round 8: *1sc into next 4 sts, 2sc into foll st; rep from * four times more. (30 sts)

Round 9: *1sc into next 5 sts, 2sc into foll st; rep from * four times more. (35 sts)

Round 10: *1sc into next 6 sts, 2sc into foll st; rep from * four times more. (40 sts)

Round 11: *1sc into next 7 sts, 2sc into foll st; rep from * four times more. (45 sts)

Round 12: *1sc into next 8 sts, 2sc into foll st; rep from * four times more. (50 sts)

Round 13: *1sc into next 9 sts, 2sc into foll st; rep from * four times more. (55 sts)

Round 14: *1sc into next 10 sts, 2sc into foll st; rep from * four times more. (60 sts)

Round 15: Work without inc.

Round 16: *1sc into next 11 sts, 2sc into foll st; rep from * four times more. (65 sts)

Round 17: Work without inc.

Round 18: *1sc into next 12 sts, 2sc into foll st; rep from *four times more. (70 sts)

Rounds 19–30: Work without inc.

Round 31: *Sc2tog, 1sc into next 8 sts; rep from * six times more. (63 sts)

Round 32: *Sc2tog, 1sc into next 7 sts; rep from * six times more. (56 sts)

Round 33: *Sc2tog, 1sc into next 6 sts; rep from * six times more. (49 sts)

Fasten off.

BODY BASE

Work in a continuous spiral. Using CC, make a yarn ring, work 6sc into the ring.

Round 1: Work 2sc into each st to end of round. (12 sts)

Round 2: *1sc into next 3sts, 2sc into foll st; rep from * three times more (15sts)

Round 3: *1sc into next 2 sts, 2sc

into foll st; rep from * four times more. (20 sts)

Round 4: *1sc into next 3 sts, 2sc into foll st; rep from * four times more. (25 sts)

Round 5: *1sc into next 4 sts, 2sc into foll st; rep from * four times more. (30 sts)

Round 6: *1sc into next 5 sts, 2sc into foll st; rep from * four times more. (35 sts)

Round 7: *1sc into next 6 sts, 2sc into foll st; rep from * four times more. (40 sts)

Round 8: *1sc into next 7 sts, 2sc into foll st; rep from * four times more. (45 sts)

Fasten off.

BACK LEGS (MAKE 2)

Work in a continuous spiral.

Using MC, make a yarn ring, work 6sc into the ring.

Round 1: *2sc into next st, 1sc; rep from * twice more. (9 sts)

Round 2: *2sc into next st, 1sc into foll 3 sts; rep from * twice more. (12 sts)

Round 3: *1sc into next 3 sts, 2sc into foll st; rep from * twice more. (15 sts)

Round 4: *1sc into next 2 sts, 2sc into foll st; rep from * four times more. (20 sts)

Round 5: *1sc into next 3 sts, 2sc into foll st; rep from * four times more. (25 sts)

Round 6: *1sc into next 4 sts, 2sc into foll st; rep from * four times more. (30 sts)

Round 7: *1sc into next 5 sts, 2sc into foll st; rep from * four times more. (35 sts)

Round 8: *1sc into next 6 sts, 2sc into foll st; rep from * four times more. (40 sts)

Round 9: *1sc into next 7 sts, 2sc into foll st; rep from * four times more. (45 sts)

Rounds 10–12: Work without inc.

Fasten off.

FEET (MAKE 2)

Work in a continuous spiral.

Using MC, make a yarn ring, work 6sc into the ring.

Round 1: *2sc into next st, 1sc; rep from * twice more. (9 sts)

Round 2: *2sc into next st, 1sc into foll 3 sts; rep from * twice more. (12 sts)

Rounds 3–8: Work without inc.

Fasten off.

FRONT LEGS (MAKE 2)

Work in a continuous spiral.

Using MC, make a yarn ring, work 6sc into the ring.

Round 1: *2sc into next st, 1sc; rep from * twice more. (9 sts)

Round 2: *2sc into next st, 1sc into foll 3 sts; rep from * twice more. (12 sts)

Round 3: *1sc into next 3 sts, 2sc into foll st; rep from * twice more. (15 sts)

Rounds 4–8: Work in sc throughout.

Round 9: *Sc2tog, 1sc into next 3 sts; rep from * six times more. (12 sts)

Rounds 10–16: Work in sc throughout.

Fasten off.

FINISHING

Brush all pieces thoroughly. Secure safety eyes, Stuff body and sew on base. Embroider nose using brown yarn. Stuff back legs slightly and sew to either side of body. Sew feet onto legs to stabilize. Sew front legs to either side of the body.

EARS (MAKE 2)

Using MC, 6ch, then fasten off. Sew to head.

TAIL

Using MC, *ch7, work 6sc along ch, then fasten off. Sew in place on body.

FINISHED SIZE: approx 6in. (15cm) long

You will need...

- 50g DK/light worsted fluffy yarn in White (MC)
- Small amount of mercerized cotton yarn in White (CC)
- E/4 (3.5mm) crochet hook
- Slicker brush
- Stuffing
- Pair of 7.5mm black safety eyes
- Small amount of yarn in Brown
- Yarn needle

abbreviations:

ch chain; **foll** following; **inc** increase; **rep** repeat; **sc** single crochet; **sc2tog** insert hook in st and draw up a loop. Insert hook in next st and draw up another loop. Yarn over, draw through all three loops on hook; **ss** slip stitch; **st(s)** stitch(es)

Penguin

This adorable emperor penguin chick is a very sociable animal. Her parents work together with the other members of their colony to feed the young, project them from predators, and shelter them from freezing winds. It's a tough job, but someone has to do it!

You will need...

- 50g fluffy yarn (such as Sirdar Blur) in Gray (MC)
- 25g same in White (A)
- 10g same in Black (B)
- Small amount of yarn in Dark Gray (C)
- E/4 (3.5mm) crochet hook
- Slicker brush
- Stuffing
- Pair 7.5mm black safety eyes
- Yarn needle

abbreviations:

ch chain; **dec** decrease; **dc2tog** yo, insert hook in st, yo, draw up loop, yo, draw through two loops on hook (leaving two loops), yo, insert hook in st, yo, draw up loop, yo, draw through two loops on hook, yo and draw through rem three loops; **foll** following; **inc** increase; **rep** repeat; **sc** single crochet; **sc2tog** insert hook in st and draw up a loop. Insert hook in next st and draw up another loop. Yo, draw through all three loops on hook; **ss** slip stitch; **st(s)** stitch(es); **tch** turning chain; **yo** yarn over

BACK HEAD AND TRIANGULAR PEAK

Using B, ch6, join with ss to make a ring. Work 6sc into center of ring.

Round 1: *2sc into each st. (12 sts)
Round 2: *1sc into next 3 sts, 2sc into foll st; rep from * twice more. (15 sts)
Round 3: *1sc into next 2 sts, 2sc into foll st; rep from * four times more. (20 sts)
Round 4: *1sc into next 3 sts, 2sc into foll st; rep from * four times more. (25 sts)
Round 5: *1sc into next 4 sts, 2sc into foll st; rep from * four times more. (30 sts)
Round 6: *1sc into next 5 sts, 2sc into foll st; rep from * four times more. (35 sts)
Round 7: *1sc into next 6 sts, 2sc into foll st; rep from * four times more. (40 sts)
Next row: 1dc into next 10 sts, 1tch, turn. (10 sts)
Next row: Dc2tog, 1dc into next 6 sts, dc2tog, 1tch, turn. (8 sts)
Next row: Work in sc throughout.
Next row: Dc2tog, 1dc into next 4 sts, dc2tog, 1tch, turn. (6 sts)
Next row: Work in sc throughout.
Next row: Dc2tog, 1dc into next 2 sts, dc2tog, 1tch, turn. (4 sts)
Next row: Work in sc throughout.
Next row: Dc2tog twice, turn. (2 sts)
Next row: Work in sc throughout.
Next row: Dc2tog. (1 st)
Fasten off.

FRONT HEAD

Using A, ch6, join with ss to make a ring. Work 6sc into center of ring.
Round 1: *2sc into each st. (12 sts)
Rounds 2–7: Work as for back head.
Fasten off.

EYE PATCHES

Using A, ch6, join with ss to make a ring. Work 6sc into center of ring.
Round 1: *2sc into each st. (12 sts)
Round 2: *1sc into next 3 sts, 2sc into foll st; rep from * twice more. (15 sts)
Round 3: *1sc into next 2 sts, 2sc into foll st; rep from * four times more. (20 sts)
Round 4: *1sc into next 3 sts, 2sc into foll st; rep from * four times more. (25 sts)
Fasten off.

BODY

Using MC, ch6, join with ss to make a ring. Work 6sc into center of the ring.
Round 1: *2sc into each st. (12 sts)
Round 2: *1sc into next 3 sts, 2sc into foll st; rep from * twice more. (15 sts)
Round 3: *1sc into next 2 sts, 2sc into foll st; rep from * four times more. (20 sts)
Round 4: *1sc into next 3 sts, 2sc into foll st; rep from * four times more. (25 sts)
Round 5: *1sc into next 4 sts, 2sc into foll st; rep from * four times more. (30 sts)

Round 6: *1sc into next 5 sts, 2sc into foll st; rep from * four times more. (35 sts)

Round 7: *1sc into next 6 sts, 2sc into foll st; rep from * four times more. (40 sts)

Round 8: *1sc into next 7 sts, 2sc into foll st; rep from * four times more. (45 sts)

Round 9: *1sc into next 8 sts, 2sc into foll st; rep from * four times more. (50 sts)

Rounds 10–13: Work without inc.

Round 14: *1sc into next 8 sts, sc2tog; rep from * to end of round. (45 sts)

Round 15: *1sc into next 7 sts, sc2tog; rep from * to end of round. (40 sts)

Round 16: *1sc into next 6 sts, sc2tog; rep from * to end of round. (35 sts)

Round 17: *1sc into next 5 sts, sc2tog; rep from * to end of round. (30 sts)

Round 18: *1sc into next 4 sts, sc2tog; rep from * to end of round. (25 sts)

Round 19: *1sc into next 3 sts, sc2tog; rep from * to end of round. (20 sts)

Fasten off.

BEAK

Work in a continuous spiral.
Using B, make a yarn ring, work 4sc into the ring.

Rows 1–4: Work without inc.
Fasten off.

FEET (MAKE 2)

Using C, *ch6, work ss into first chain; rep from * twice more.
Fasten off.

WINGS (MAKE 2)

Using MC, 6ch.

Rows 1–6: Work without inc. (5 sts)

Row 7: Sc2tog, 1sc into next st, sc2tog. (3 sts)

Row 8: Sc3tog. (1 st)
Fasten off.

FINISHING

Brush all pieces vigorously with a slicker brush. Sew back head to front head, overlapping the triangular piece and sewing into place to form a peak at the front head. Sew eye patches in place either side of the peak. Insert plastic eyes through center of eye patches. Sew beak to tip of triangular peak.

Stuff head then stuff the body and stitch to head. Sew wings in place to body. Sew feet at base of body.

FINISHED SIZE: approx 4in. (10cm) high

Turtles

These little critters have just hatched on a Queensland beach and now face the long swim north to meet the rest of the family. Some of the lazier ones have a cunning plan; to use their shells as boats and float their way across the ocean, so they're not too tired for the big welcome home party.

HEAD

Work in a continuous spiral.

Using A, ch6 join with ss to make a ring.

Row 1: Work 6sc into center of ring.

Row 2: 2sc into each st to end of round. (12 sts)

Row 3: 1sc in each st to end of round.

Fasten off.

MOUTH

Using D, make a yarn ring, work 6sc into center of ring.

Fasten off.

JAW

Using A, ch6, join with ss to make a ring.

Fasten off.

UNDERSHELL

Work in a continuous spiral.

Using B, make a yarn ring, work 6sc into the ring.

Round 1: 1sc in each st to end of round. (6 sts)

Round 2: 2sc into each st to end. (12 sts)

Round 3: *1sc, 2sc into foll st; rep from * five times more. (18 sts)

Fasten off.

LEGS (MAKE 4)

Work in a continuous spiral.

Using A, make a yarn ring, work 6sc into the ring.

Round 1: 1sc in each st to end of round. (6 sts)

Rounds 2–6: Work without inc. (6 sts)

Fasten off.

SHELL

Work in a continuous spiral.

Using B, ch3, join with a ss to make a ring.

Row 1: Work 10dc into center of the ring.

Do not fasten off.

Change to C.

Row 2: Ch3 (counts as dc), 2dc in same st, dc behind post in next dc, *3dc in next dc, dc behind post in next st; rep from * to end of round. Join with ss. (24 sts)

Change to B.

Row 3: Ch1, sc into each st to end, join with ss. (24 sts)

Fasten off.

FINISHING

Sew bead eyes or safety eyes onto either side of head. Stuff head lightly, then sew pink mouth to underside of head. Sew green jaw over pink mouth to create bottom jaw. Sew head onto shell. Sew legs to undershell to form an X shape. Sew undershell to shell leaving a small gap. Stuff lightly. Sew remaining seam. Work in all ends and trim.

FINISHED SIZE: approx 2½in. (6cm) long

Crocodile

It's a little known fact that crocodiles love a bit of Elton John... they've heard his music isn't bad either! This crocheted croc has a big smile, most likely because he's spotted his next meal swimming down the river.

TAIL, BODY, AND HEAD

Using MC, ch6, join with ss to make a ring. Work 6sc into center of the ring

Round 1: 1sc into each st to end of round. (6 sts)

Round 2: *2sc into next st, 1sc into foll st; rep from * twice more. (9 sts)

Round 3: 1sc into each st to end of round. (9 sts)

Round 4: *2sc into next st, 1sc into foll 2 sts; rep from * to end of round. (12 sts)

Round 5: 1sc into each st to end of round. (12 sts)

Round 6: *2sc into next st, 1sc into foll 3 sts; rep from * to end of round. (15 sts)

Rounds 7–17: 1sc into each st to end of round. (15 sts)

Round 18: *2sc into next st, 1sc into foll 2 sts; rep from * to end of round. (20 sts)

Round 19: 1sc into each st to end of round. (20 sts)

Round 20: *2sc into next st, 1sc into foll 3 sts; rep from * to end of round. (25 sts)

Round 21: 1sc into each st to end of round. (25 sts)

Round 22: *2sc into next st, 1sc into foll 4 sts; rep from * to end of round. (30 sts)

Rounds 23–35: 1sc into each st to end of round. (30 sts)

Round 36: *1sc into next 4 sts, sc2tog; rep from * to end of round. (25 sts)

Round 37: *1sc into next 3 sts, sc2tog; rep from * to end of round. (20 sts)

Round 38: 1sc into each st to end of round. (20 sts)

Round 39: *2sc into next st, 1sc into foll 3 sts; rep from * to end of round. (25 sts)

Round 40: *2sc into next st, 1sc into foll 12 sts, 2sc into next st, 1sc into foll 11 sts. (27 sts)

Rounds 41–44: 1sc into each st to end of round. (27 sts)

Round 45: 1sc into next 2 sts, mark last st, 1sc into foll 11 sts, mark last st, work 1sc into foll 2 sts sc2tog to end of round. (21 sts)

Round 46: 1sc into each st to end of round. (21 sts)

Fasten off.

TOP JAW

Using MC, work 10sc into sts between markers on top side of body.

Row 1: Sc2tog, 1sc into foll 6 sts, sc2tog. (8 sts)

Rows 2–12: 1sc into each st to end of row. Fasten off.

Using MC and starting at right side of top jaw work 13sc along side edge, 8sc along top edge, 13sc along side edge. Do not work tch, turn. (34 sts)

Next row: *1sc into each st to end of row. Do not work tch, turn.

Repeat from * twice more. (30 sts)

Fasten off.

BOTTOM JAW

Insert hook into first st to the left side of top jaw to make the first sc, work as for top jaw.

You will need...

- 25g DK/light worsted yarn in Green (MC)
- 10g same in Pink (A)
- 10g same in White (B)
- E/4 (3.5mm) crochet hook
- Stuffing
- Pair of 7.5mm safety cat's eyes
- Pipe cleaners
- Yarn needle

abbreviations

ch chain; **foll** following; **inc** increase; **picot st** ch3 ss in next st; **rep** repeat; **sc** single crochet; **sc2tog** insert hook in st and draw up loop. Insert hook in next st and draw up another loop. Yo, draw through all three loops on hook; **ss** slip stitch; **st(s)** stitch(es); **tch** turning chain

INSIDE MOUTH

Using A, ch11.

Rows 1–24: 1sc into 10 sts, 1tch, turn. (10 sts)
Fasten off.

FRONT LEGS AND FEET (MAKE 2)

Work in a continuous spiral.

Using MC, ch8. join with ss to make a ring.

Rounds 1–10: 1sc into each st. (8 sts)

Round 11: sc2tog five times. (4 sts)

Work 1sc into next 2 sts.

Using CC, *ch5, 4sc along ch, ss into st at base of 5-ch; rep from * once more, ch5, 4sc along ch, ss into next st.

Fasten off.

BACK LEGS AND FEET (MAKE 2)

Work in a continuous spiral.

Using MC, ch10, join with ss to make a ring.

Rounds 1–2: 1sc into each st. (10 sts)

Round 3: *Sc2tog, 1sc into foll 3 sts; rep from * once more. (8 sts)

Rounds 4–14: 1sc into each st. (8 sts)

Round 15: Sc2tog five times. (4 sts)

Work 1sc into next 2 sts.

Using CC, *ch5, 4sc along ch, ss into st at base of 5-ch; rep from * once more, ch5, 4sc along ch, ss into next st.

Fasten off.

FINISHING

Secure safety eyes in place in head over sc2tog sts on top of body. Stuff the body, inserting a pipe cleaner if desired. Stuff the jaw sparingly and shape a pipe cleaner around each piece to keep the jaw shape. Sew inside mouth piece in place stretching it between the top and bottom jaw.

Insert a trimmed pipe cleaner through the center of each leg and stuff. Sew to body using photograph on page 43 as a guide. Sew a large stitch over top and bottom of both eyes to represent eye lids.

NOSTRILS (MAKE 2)

Using MC, 6ch and fasten off.

Sew to end of nose.

BACK RIDGES

Working either side of 5 center back sts, work a row of 12sc 2 sts down the body towards tail end.

Moving across towards the center back by 1 st, work a further 4sc.

Moving towards the center back by another st, work a further 17sc.

Fasten off.

Rep for second ridge.

FINISHED SIZE: approx 10in. (25cm) long

Frogs and toads

Great little treats for Halloween, these little toads are very easy to make! According to Wikipedia, "any distinction between frogs and toads is irrelevant," so you can call these little darlings what you want!

BODY TOP

Work in a continuous spiral.

Using MC, make a yarn ring, work 8sc into the ring.

Round 1: 1sc in each st to end of round. (8 sts)

Round 2: 2sc into each st to end of round. (16 sts)

Round 3: *2sc in next st, 1sc in foll 3 sts; rep from * three times more. (20 sts)

Round 4: *2sc in next st, 1sc in foll 2 sts; rep from * five times more, 1sc into next 2sts (26 sts)

Round 5: *2sc in next st, 1sc into foll 3 sts; rep from * four times more, 1sc into next st. (32 sts) **

Round 6: Work in sc throughout.
Fasten off.

BELLY

Using CC, ch8, join with ss to make a ring. Work as for body to **.

Rounds 6–11: Work in sc throughout.
Fasten off.

LEGS (MAKE 2)

Work in a continuous spiral.

Using MC, make a yarn ring, work 8sc into the ring.

Round 1: 1sc into each st to end of round. (8 sts)

Round 2: 2sc into each st to end of round. (16 sts)

Round 3: *2sc in next st, 1sc in foll 3 sts; rep from * three times more. (20 sts)

Round 4: Work in sc throughout.
Do not fasten off, ch4 then CL4 to make a toe, rep twice starting in the same spot.

FINISHING

Sew bead eyes or safety eyes onto head. Sew together the head and body leaving a small gap. Stuff. Sew remaining seam, Stitch legs onto body, using the photograph on page 44 as a guide. Pinch head and body to accentuate mouth, then use pink yarn to sew together to secure. For warts on toad, CL4 into 2 rows on back.

FINISHED SIZE: approx 2in. (5cm) long

You will need...

- 10g Aran weight/worsted yarn in Green (MC)
- 5g DK/light worsted yarn in Bamboo or White (CC)
- E/4 (3.5mm) crochet hook
- 10mm safety eyes or 2 small black beads
- Stuffing
- Pink embroidery thread
- Yarn needle

abbreviations:

ch chain; **CL4** insert hook into st, yarn over, draw loop through, rep into next st (3 loops on hook), rep into next st (4 loops on hook), rep into next st (5 loops on hook), yarn over, draw through all 5 loops on hook; **foll** following; **inc** increase; **rep** repeat; **sc** single crochet; **ss** slip stitch; **st(s)** stitch(es)

Walrus

Ever wondered why a walrus has such big tusks? They use them for several things, including digging holes in the ice so they can hunt for food, and dragging themselves out of the water once full. They are also notorious show-offs, using their tusks to display to females and attract a mate.

You will need...

- 50g DK/light worsted yarn in Gray (MC)
- 10g same in White (CC)
- E/4 (3.5mm) crochet hook
- Stuffing
- Two 4mm round black bead eyes
- Yarn needle

abbreviations:

ch chain; **foll** following; **inc** increase; **rep** repeat; **sc** single crochet; **ss** slip stitch; **st(s)** stitch(es); **tr** triple crochet

HEAD AND UPPER BODY
Using MC, ch6, join with ss to make a ring.
Round 1: *2sc into next st, 1sc into foll st; rep from * twice more. (9 sts)
Rounds 2–3: Work without inc.
Round 4: *2sc into next st, 1sc into foll 2 sts; rep from * twice more. (12 sts)
Rounds 5–6: Work without inc.
Round 7: *2sc into next st, 1sc into foll st; rep from * five times more. (18 sts)
Rounds 8–9: Work without inc.
Round 10: *2sc into next st, 1sc into foll 2 sts; rep from * five times more. (24 sts)
Round 11: *2sc into next st, 1sc into foll 3 sts; rep from * five times more. (30 sts)
Round 12: *2sc into next st, 1sc into foll 4 sts; rep from * five times more. (36 sts)
Round 13: *2sc into next st, 1sc into foll 5 sts; rep from * five times more. (42 sts)
Round 14: *2sc into next st, 1sc into foll 6 sts; rep from * five times more. (48 sts)
Rounds 15–24: Work without inc.
Fasten off.

LOWER BODY
Using MC, ch6, join with ss to make a ring.
Rounds 1–4: 1sc into each st. (6 sts)
Round 5: *2sc into next st, 1sc into foll st; rep from * twice more. (9 sts)
Rounds 6–7: Work without inc.

Round 8: *2sc into next st, 1sc into foll 2 sts; rep from * twice more. (12 sts)
Rounds 9–10: Work without inc.
Round 11: *2sc into next st, 1sc into foll st; rep from * five times more. (18 sts)
Rounds 12–13: Work without inc.
Round 14: *2sc into next st, 1sc into foll 2 sts; rep from * five times more. (24 sts)
Round 15: *2sc into next st, 1sc into foll 3 sts; rep from * five times more. (30 sts)
Round 16: *2sc into next st, 1sc into foll 4 sts; rep from * five times more. (36 sts)
Round 17: *2sc into next st, 1sc into foll 5 sts; rep from * five times more. (42 sts)
Round 18: *2sc into next st, 1sc into foll 6 sts; rep from * five times more. (48 sts)
Rounds 19–20: Work without inc.
Fasten off.

TAIL
Flatten the tip of the tail slightly, then join in yarn by inserting the hook through both layers of fabric at the tip of the

lower body, *ch3, 5tr into the base of the ch, ch3, 1sc into the base of the ch; rep from * once more.
Fasten off.

NOSE
Using MC, ch6, join with ss to make a ring.
Rounds 1–3: 1sc into each st.
Fasten off.

TUSKS (MAKE 2)
Using CC, ch4, join with ss to make a ring.
Rounds 1–16: 1sc into each st, working into back loop of st only.
Fasten off.

FLIPPER (MAKE 2)
Using MC, ch6, join with ss to make a ring.
Rounds 1–3: 1sc into each st.
Round 4: *2sc into next st, 1sc into foll st; rep from * twice more. (9 sts)
Round 5: *2sc into next st, 1sc into foll 2 sts; rep from * twice more. (12 sts)
Round 6: *2sc into next st, 1sc into foll 5 sts; rep from * once more. (14 sts)
Round 7: *2sc into next st, 1sc into foll 6 sts; rep from * once more. (16 sts)
Rounds 8–14: Work without inc.
Fasten off.

FINISHING
Secure bead eyes to the head end of upper body. Sew body pieces together and stuff to create walrus shape. Sew nose onto upper body and sew tusks underneath. Sew the open end of the each flipper closed and sew to the upper body.

FINISHED SIZE: approx 9in. (22.5cm) long

Manta ray

Manta rays are gentle giants, the biggest of the rays. They sweep through oceans, scooping up plankton and fish, before pulling up to the manta wash, where little fishes provide a spring-clean for a free meal. Mantas are clever and very curious, even popping out of the water to take a look at our world. If you love *Finding Nemo*, you might also know they make excellent teachers.

You will need...

- 25g of DK/light worsted yarn in Dark Blue (MC)
- 25g of same in White (CC)
- E/4 (3.5mm) crochet hook
- Stuffing
- Pair of 10mm safety eyes
- Scrap of pink felt
- Yarn needle
- Pipe cleaners

abbreviations:

ch chain; **foll** following; **inc** increase; **rep** repeat; **sc** single crochet; **ss** slip stitch; **st(s)** stitch(es); **tch** turning chain

UPPER BODY

Using MC, ch10 plus one tch.
Working back and forth in rows.
Row 1: Sc into the 2nd ch from the hook, sc each ch to the end, 1tch. (10 sts)
Rows 2–4: Sc in each st, 1tch. (10 sts)
Row 5: 2sc into next st, sc into foll 8 sts, 2sc into last st, 1tch. (12 sts)
Rows 6–25: 2sc into next st, sc into each foll st to last st, 2sc into last st, 1tch. (62 sts)
Fasten off.

UPPER TAIL

With the fastening off tail from the upper body to the right, fold body in half and mark center point with a scrap of yarn. Using MC, begin working into back edge of body 4 sts to the right of center point.
Row 1: Sc into each of 8 sts along edge, 1tch. (8 sts)
Rows 2–4: Sc into each st, 1tch.
Rows 5–11: Sc into each st, do not use tch so each row reduces by one st. (1 st)
Ch22.
Fasten off.

LOWER BODY

Using CC, ch10 plus one tch.
Working back and forth in rows.
Row 1: Sc into the 2nd ch from the hook, sc each ch to the end, 1tch. (10 sts)

Rows 2–4: Sc in each st, 1tch. (10 sts)
Row 5: 2sc into next st, sc into foll 8 sts, 2sc into last st, 1tch. (12 sts)
Rows 6–25: 2sc into next st, sc into each foll st to last st, 2sc into last st, 1tch. (62 sts)
Fasten off.

LOWER TAIL

With the fastening off tail from the lower body to the right, fold body in half and mark center point with a scrap of yarn. Using CC, begin working into back edge of body 4 sts to the right of center point.
Row 1: Sc into each of 8 sts along edge, 1tch. (8 sts)
Rows 2–4: Sc into each st, 1tch.
Rows 5–11: Sc into each st, do not use tch so each row reduces by one st. (1 st)
Ch22.
Fasten off.

FINISHING

Work 1 row of sc around tail, wings and mouth, to give a smooth edge. This also thickens tail and makes it one crochet stitch wide. Secure safety eyes and stitch outlines in CC. Sew a piece of pink felt onto the inside of each mouth part. Sew a pipe cleaner in a T-shape on the edges of the wing and tail. Stuff and sew the edges together, leaving the mouth open for a happy expression.

FINISHED SIZE: approx 8in. (20cm) long

Squid

A squid has very specialized skin that can change color to match its surroundings. This is particularly useful when there's a predator nearby or if trying to catch food and wanting to stay out of sight. It looks like this squid still has a lot to learn though, because his bright orange color definitely makes him stand out in a crowd.

SQUID TOP AND TENTACLES

Work in a continuous spiral.
Using MC, make a yarn ring, work 6sc into the ring.
Rounds 1–2: Sc in each st. (6 sts)
Round 3: *Sc into next st, 2sc into foll st; rep from * twice more. (9 sts)
Round 4: *Sc into each of next 2 sts, 2sc into foll st; rep from * twice more. (12 sts)
Round 5: *Sc into each of next 3 sts, 2sc into foll st; rep from * twice more. (15 sts)
Round 6: *Sc into each of next 4 sts, 2sc into foll st; rep from * twice more. (18 sts)
Round 7: *Sc into each of next 5 sts, 2sc into foll st; rep from * twice more. (21 sts)
Rounds 8–28: Work without inc.
Round 29: *Sc into each of next 3 sts, ch25, skip first ch, sc back along 24 ch; rep from * six times more.
Fasten off.

SQUID BASE

Work in a continuous spiral.
Using MC, make a yarn ring, work 6sc into the ring.
Rounds 1–2: Sc in each st. (6 sts)
Round 3: *Sc into next st, 2sc into foll st; rep from * twice more. (9 sts)
Round 4: *Sc into each of next 2 sts, 2sc into foll st; rep from * twice more. (12 sts)
Round 5: *Sc into each of next 3 sts, 2sc into foll st; rep from * twice more. (15 sts)
Round 6: *Sc into each of next 4 sts, 2sc into foll st; rep from * twice more. (18 sts)
Round 7: *Sc into each of next 5 sts, 2sc into foll st; rep from * twice more. (21 sts)
Fasten off.

FINISHING

Secure safety eyes to head. Stuff the squid top and sew on the base.

FINISHED SIZE: approx 9in. (22.5cm) long

You will need...

- 25g DK/light worsted yarn in Orange
- E/4 (3.5mm) crochet hook
- Pair of 15mm safety eyes
- Stuffing
- Yarn needle

abbreviations:

ch chain; **inc** increase; **foll** following; **rep** repeat; **sc** single crochet; **ss** slip stitch; **st(s)** stitch(es); **tch** turning chain

Whale

Whales are by far the largest creatures in the sea. Many species communicate through whale song, having come to rely on sound for feeding as their sense of smell and sight are restricted underwater. This crocheted sperm whale also uses its tail to communicate, slapping it against the water to attract attention.

You will need...

- 25g DK/light worsted yarn in Blue
- E/4 (3.5mm) crochet hook
- Pair of 15mm safety eyes
- Yarn needle

abbreviations:

ch chain; inc increase; foll following; rep repeat; sc single crochet; sc2tog insert hook in st and draw up a loop. Insert hook in next st and draw up another loop. Yarn over, draw through all three loops on hook; ss slip stitch; st(s) stitch(es); tr triple crochet

BODY

The body is made in two parts.
Ch6, join with ss to make a ring.
Round 1: 2sc in each st. (12 sts)
Round 2: *Sc in next st, 2sc into foll st; rep from * five times more. (18 sts)
Round 3: *Sc into each of next 2 sts, 2sc into foll st; rep from * five times more. (24 sts)
Round 4: *Sc into each of next 3 sts, 2sc into foll st; rep from * five times more. (30 sts)
Round 5: *Sc into each of next 4 sts, 2sc into foll st; rep from * five times more. (36 sts)
Round 6: *Sc into each of next 5 sts, 2sc into foll st; rep from * five times more. (42 sts)
Round 7: *Sc into each of next 6 sts, 2sc into foll st; rep from * five times more. (48 sts)
Round 8: *Sc into each of next 7 sts, 2sc into foll st; rep from * five times more. (54 sts)
Rounds 9–15: Work without inc.
Round 16: *Sc into each of next 7 sts, sc2tog; rep from * five times more. (48 sts)
Round 17: *Sc into each of next 6 sts, sc2tog; rep from * five times more. (42 sts)
Fasten off.

BODY BASE

Ch6, join with ss to make a ring.
Round 1: 2sc in each st. (12 sts)
Round 2: *Sc in next st, 2sc into foll st; rep from * five times more. (18 sts)
Round 3: *Sc into each of next 2 sts, 2sc into foll st; rep from * five times more. (24 sts)
Round 4: *Sc into each of next 3 sts, 2sc into foll st; rep from * five times more. (30 sts)
Round 5: *Sc into each of next 4 sts, 2sc into foll st; rep from * five times more. (36 sts)
Round 6: *Sc into each of next 5 sts, 2sc into foll st; rep from * five times more. (42 sts)
Fasten off.

TAIL

Ch6, join with ss to make a ring.
Round 1: 2sc in each st. (12 sts)
Rounds 2–3: Work without inc.
Round 4: *Sc in next st, 2sctog; rep from * twice more. (9 sts)
Round 5: *Sc in next st, 2sctog; rep from * twice more. (6 sts)
Rounds 6–8: Work without inc.
Flatten the tip of the tail slightly, then join in yarn by inserting the hook through both layers of fabric at the tip of the tail, *ch3, 5tr into the base of the ch, ch3, 1sc into the base of the ch; rep from * once more.
Fasten off.

FINISHING

Secure safety eyes on each side of head. Stuff top and sew on base. Sew tail on and embroider mouth, using the photograph on page 55 as a guide.

FINISHED SIZE: approx 4in. (10cm) long

Shrimp

A touch of Salvador Dali-inspired surrealism surrounds this jumbo shrimp. Made with thick pink yarn and big button eyes, this little crustacean looks good enough to eat. Make a whole shoal in different shades of pink and you will have your own seafood cocktail!

HEAD AND BODY

Ch6, join with ss to make a ring.

Rounds 1–2: Sc into each st.

Round 3: *Sc into next st, 2sc into foll st; rep from * twice more. (9 sts)

Round 4: *Sc into each of next 2 sts, 2sc into foll st; rep from * twice more. (12 sts)

Round 5: *Sc into each of next 3 sts, 2sc into foll st; rep from * twice more. (15 sts)

Round 6: *Sc into each of next 4 sts, 2sc into foll st; rep from * twice more. (18 sts)

Round 7: *Sc into each of next 5 sts, 2sc into foll st; rep from * twice more. (21 sts)

Secure safety eyes.

Rounds 8–19: Work without inc.

Rounds 20–42: 1dc in each st. (21 sts)

Round 43: *Dc into each of next 5 sts, dc2tog; rep from * twice more. (18 sts)

Round 44: *Dc into each of next 4 sts, dc2tog; rep from * twice more. (15 sts)

Stuff body.

Round 45: *Sc into each of next 3 sts, sc2tog; rep from * twice more. (12 sts)

Round 46: *Sc into next 2 sts, sc2tog; rep from * twice more. (9 sts)

Round 47: Work without dec.

Fasten off.

Flatten the tip of the tail slightly, then join in yarn by inserting the hook through both layers of fabric at the tip of the tail, *ch3, 5tr into the base of the ch, ch3, 1sc into the base of the ch; rep from * once more.

Fasten off.

ANTENNA (MAKE 2)

Crochet tightly, so the antennae are stiff.

Ch6, join with ss to make a ring.

Rounds 1–10: Sc into each st.

Fasten off.

FINISHING

Join yarn to the side of the body using the photograph on page 56 as a guide for position of legs, then crochet into the body placing the last leg slightly higher, *ch18 then crochet back into body next to the base, rep from * three times more.

FINISHED SIZE: approx 8in. (20cm) high

You will need...

- 50g Chunky yarn in Pink
- H/8 (5mm) crochet hook
- Pair of 15mm safety eyes
- Stuffing
- Yarn needle

abbreviations:

ch chain; **dc** double crochet; **dc2tog** Yo, insert hook in st, yo, draw up a loop, yo, draw through two loops on hook (leaving two loops), yo, insert hook in st, yo, draw up a loop, yo, draw through two loops on hook, yo and draw through remaining three loops; **dec** decrease; **inc** increase; **rep** repeat; **sc** single crochet; **sc2tog** insert hook in st and draw up a loop. Insert hook in next st and draw up another loop. Yo, draw through all three loops on hook; **ss** slip stitch; **st(s)** stitch(es); **tch** turning chain; **yo** yarn over

Duck-billed platypus

The platypus is a pretty unique animal that can only be found in the rivers and streams of Eastern Australia. When it was first discovered nature experts studying pictures of the animal thought it was a hoax, due to its duck bill, tail like a beaver, and venomous spur on the back leg. It may be unusual looking, but it certainly has a lot of character.

You will need...

- 25g DK/light worsted yarn in Light Brown (MC)
- 25g same in Dark Brown (CC)
- E/4 (3.5mm) crochet hook
- Pair of 5mm black safety eyes
- Stuffing
- Yarn needle

abbreviations:

ch chain; **foll** following; **inc** increase; **rep** repeat; **sc** single crochet; **sc2tog** insert hook in st and draw up a loop. Insert hook in next st and draw up another loop. Yarn over, draw through all three loops on hook; **ss** slip stitch; **st(s)** stitch(es)

HEAD AND BODY

Using CC, ch6, join with ss to make a ring.
Round 1: 2sc into each st. (12 sts)
Round 2: *2sc into next st, sc into foll st; rep from * five more times. (18 sts)
Rounds 3–8: Work without inc.
Change to MC.
Round 9: *2sc into next st, sc into each of foll 2 sts; rep from * five more times. (24 sts)
Rounds 10–30: Work without inc.
Secure safety eyes and stuff body.
Round 31: *Sc2tog, sc into each of foll 2 sts; rep from * five more times. (18 sts)
Round 32: *Sc2tog, sc into foll st; rep from * five more times. (12 sts)
Rounds 33–38: Work without inc.
Round 39: Sc2tog six times. (6 sts)
Fasten off.

FEET (MAKE 4)

Using CC, join yarn to body, *ch8, ss into first st, rep from * twice more.
Rep once more for each foot.
Fasten off.

FINISHING

Secure safety eyes, stuff head and body, sew up final seam.

FINISHED SIZE: approx 8in. (20cm) long

Animals from afar

African land snail

African land snails have developed a bad reputation because of their tremendous appetite. If you get a group together they can demolish entire crops in less than a day—and have even been banned in America in case they escape into the wild. If you choose to make one, be sure you keep a close eye on him so he doesn't break loose and start munching on all the plants in your home.

You will need...

- 50g Chunky yarn in Pink (MC)
- 25g same in Light Blue (A)
- 25g same in Dark Blue (B)
- E/4 (3.5mm) crochet hook
- Stuffing
- Pair of 5mm black beads
- Yarn needle

abbreviations:

ch chain; dc double crochet; foll following; inc increase; rep repeat; sc single crochet; sc2tog insert hook in st and draw up a loop. Insert hook in next st and draw up another loop. Yarn over, draw through all three loops on hook; ss slip stitch; st(s) stitch(es)

SHELL (MAKE 2)

Work alternate rounds in A and B.
Work in a continuous spiral.
Using A, make a yarn ring, work 12dc into the ring.
Round 1: Using B, ch3 (counts as first dc), 1dc into st at base of 3-ch, 2dc into each st to end of round. (24 sts)
Round 2: Using A, ch3 (counts as first dc) *2dc into next two sts, 1dc into foll st; rep from * to end of round. (40 sts)
Round 3: Using B, ch3(counts as first dc) *2dc into next st, 1dc in foll 2 sts; rep from * to end of round. (53 sts)
Round 4: Using A, 1dc into every st to end of round.
Fasten off.

BODY

Using MC, ch6, join with ss to make a ring.
Round 1: Work 6sc into center of ring.
Round 2: 2sc each st to end of round. (12 sts)
Round 3: *2sc into next st, 1sc into foll st; rep from * to end of round. (18 sts)
Rounds 4–21: 1sc into every st to end of round.
Round 22: 1sc into next 2 sts, *sc2tog, 1sc into foll 2 sts; rep from * to end of round. (14 sts)

Round 23: 1sc into next 2 sts, *sc2tog, 1sc into foll 2 sts; rep from * to end. (11 sts)
Place last st on a stitch holder.
Stuff body.
Place held st back onto crochet hook.
Round 24: 1sc into next st, *sc2tog, 1sc into foll 2 sts; rep from * once more, sc2tog. (8 sts)
Round 25: *Sc2tog, 1sc into next 2 sts; rep from * to end. (6 sts)
Round 26: *Sc2tog; rep from * twice more. (3 sts)
Round 27: Sc3tog.
Fasten off.

FINISHING

Sew the two sides of the shell together leaving a small opening. Stuff, then complete the seam. Sew the shell to the body.

ANTENNA (MAKE 2)

Using MC, ch8.
Fasten off.
Sew antennae to top of head. Sew a bead to the end of each chain.

FINISHED SIZE: approx 10in. (25cm) long

Crochet the antennae as firmly as you can. They need to be stiff so they will stand up nice and straight. Alternatively, you can insert a pipe cleaner inside when they are complete—and this will allow you to position the antennae in a curve as shown on the left.

For a small child, it may be better to omit the black beads and embroider the eyes in black embroidery thread instead. This will avoid any risk of a bead coming off if the snail is chewed!

This is a cute toy for a baby, in which case you might like to include a small bell or rattle inside the shell. Make sure there is no danger that it can come out through the stitches.

Make several of these cute snails in different colors and have your own snail farm!

Flamingo

It's not known quite why flamingos stand on one leg, but some scientists suggest it's because they have the ability to let one side of their body go to sleep while the other is still awake. For this flamingo the reason is completely different—she is an expert hopscotch player and is in training for her next tournament.

BODY AND HEAD

Using A, ch4 join with ss to make a ring.

Rounds 1–3: 1sc into each st to end of round.

Round 4: *1sc into next st, 2sc into foll st; rep from * once more. (6 sts)

Round 5: *1sc into next 2 sts, 2sc into foll st; rep from * once more. (8 sts)

Rounds 6–8: 1sc into each st to end of round. Change to MC.

Round 9: 1sc into each st to end of round. (8 sts)

Round 10: *1sc into next 3 sts, 2sc into foll st; rep from * once more. (10 sts)

Round 11: 1sc into each st to end of round. (10 sts)

Round 12: *1sc into next 4 sts, 2sc into foll st; rep from * once more. (12 sts)

Rounds 13–14: 1sc into each st to end of round. (12 sts)

Round 15: *1sc into next 3 sts, sc2tog; rep from * once more. (10 sts)

Rounds 16–35: 1sc into each st to end of round. (10 sts)

Round 36: *1sc into next st, 2sc into foll st; rep from * to end of round. (15 sts)

Round 37: *1sc into next 2 sts, 2sc into foll st; rep from * to end of round. (20 sts)

Round 38: *1sc into next 3 sts, 2sc into foll st; rep from * to end of round. (25 sts)

Round 39: *1sc into next 4 sts, 2sc into foll st; rep from * to end of round. (30 sts)

Round 40: *1sc into next 14 sts, 2sc into foll st; rep from * once more. (32 sts)

Rounds 41–50: 1sc into each st to end of round. (32 sts)

Round 51: *1sc into next 14 sts, sc2tog; rep from * once more. (30 sts)

Round 52: *1sc into next 4 sts, sc2tog; rep from * to end of round. (25 sts)

Round 53: *1sc into next 3 sts, sc2tog; rep from * to end of round. (20 sts)

Round 54: *1sc into next 2 sts, sc2tog; rep from * to end of round. (15 sts)
Stuff body.

Round 55: *1sc into next 3 sts, sc2tog; rep from * to end of round. (12 sts)

Round 56: Sc2tog to end of round. (6 sts)
Fasten off.

LEGS (MAKE 2)

Work in a continuous spiral.

Using B, ch6 join with ss to make a ring. Work 6sc into center of the ring.

Rounds 1–32: 1sc into each st to end of round. (6 sts)
Fasten off.

Ch10, secure in first chain, ch10, secure in first chain, ch10, secure in first chain.

FEET (MAKE 2)

Work as for legs for 10 rows.
Fasten off.

You will need...

- 25g DK/light worsted yarn in Pink (MC)
- 5g same in Brown (A)
- Small amount of yarn in Orange (B)
- Small amount of yarn in White (C)
- E/4 (3.5mm) crochet hook
- Stuffing
- 2 small black beads, or safety eyes
- 3 pipe cleaners for neck and body
- Yarn needle

abbreviations:

ch chain; **foll** following; **inc** increase; **rep** repeat; **sc** single crochet; **sc2tog** insert hook in st and draw up a loop. Insert hook in next st and draw up another loop. Yarn over, draw through all three loops on hook; **ss** slip stitch; **st(s)** stitch(es); **tr** triple

UPPER WING (MAKE 2)

Using MC, ch6, join with ss to make a ring.

Row 1: 4ch (counts as tr), 9tr into center of ring, turn.

Row 2: 4ch (counts as tr), 1tr into st at base of 3-ch, 2tr into each foll st to end of round. (20 sts)

Fasten off.

UNDER WING (MAKE 2)

Using C, ch6 join with ss to make a ring.

Row 1: 4ch (counts as tr), 9tr into center of ring, turn.

Row 2: 3ch (counts as dc), 1dc into st at base of 3-ch, 2dc into each foll st to end of round. (20 sts).

Fasten off.

FINISHING

Insert pipe cleaner through neck. Sew bead or safety eyes onto head, then stuff head and body. Sew up open end of body. Sew wings in place on upper side of body, placing the under wings closest to the body. Insert pipe cleaner into legs and sew legs onto underside of body. Insert sewing needle through the foot piece between rows 5 and 6. Sew feet to legs in a cross shape approx 1in. (2.5cm) from end.

FINISHED SIZE: approx 10in. (25cm) long

Tortoise

Tortoises can live to a ripe old age, with records suggesting the oldest, Jonathan—a Seychelles Giant tortoise—is over 170 years old. If the crocheted one here doesn't hurry up and cross the road, it's pretty unlikely he will get anywhere near that!

You will need...

- 25g DK/light worsted yarn in Green (MC)
- 10g same in Dark Green (A)
- 5g same in Pink (B)
- E/4 (3.5mm) crochet hook
- Stuffing
- Pair of 5mm safety eyes
- Yarn needle

abbreviations:

ch chain; dc double crochet; foll following; inc increase; rep repeat; sc single crochet; sc2tog insert hook in st and draw up a loop. Insert hook in next st and draw up another loop. Yarn over, draw through all three loops on hook; ss slip stitch; st(s) stitch(es)

SHELL

Using MC, ch12, join with ss to make a ring.

Round 1: 1dc into each st, join with ss. (12 sts)

Round 2: Ch3 (counts as a st), 1dc into st at base of 3-ch, 2dc into each st to end of round, join with ss. (24 sts)

Round 3: Ch3, (counts as a st),1dc into st at base of 3-ch, *2dc in next two sts, 1dc in foll st; rep from * to end. (38 sts)

Rounds 4–5: Work in sc without inc.

Rounds 6–7: Ch1, work in sc throughout.
Fasten off.

BODY BASE

Using MC, ch12, join with ss to make a ring.

Round 1: 1dc into each st, join with ss. (12 sts)

Round 2: Ch3 (counts as a st), 1dc into st at base of 3-ch, 2dc into each st to end of round, join with a slip st. (24 sts)

Round 3: Ch3, (counts as a st), 1dc into st at base of 3-ch, *2dc in next two sts, 1dc in foll st; rep from * to end. (38 sts)

Round 4: Ch1, work in sc throughout
Fasten off.

LEGS (MAKE 4)

Work in a continuous spiral.

Using A, make a yarn ring, work 8sc into the ring.

Round 1: 1sc into each st. (8 sts)

Rounds 2–10: Work without inc.
Fasten off.

HEAD

Work in a continuous spiral.

Using A, make a yarn ring, work 6sc into the ring.

Round 1: 2sc into each st to end of round. (12 sts)

Round 2: *1sc into next st, 2sc into foll st; rep from * twice more. (15 sts)

Round 3: *1sc into next 2 sts, 2sc into foll st; rep from * four times more. (20 sts)

Round 4: *1sc into next 3 sts, 2sc into foll st; rep from * four times more. (25 sts)

Round 5: Work without inc. (25 sts)
Fasten off.

INSIDE MOUTH

Work in a continuous spiral.

Using B, make a yarn ring, work 6sc into the ring.

Round 1: 2sc into each st to end of round. (12 sts)

Round 2: *2sc in next st, 1sc in foll st; rep from * to end of round. (18 sts)

Round 3: *2sc in next st, 1sc in foll 2 sts; rep from * to end of round. (24 sts)
Fasten off.

JAW

Work in a continuous spiral.
Using A, make a yarn ring, work 6sc into the ring.
Round 1: 2sc in each st. (12 sts)
Fasten off.

FINISHING

Stuff shell. Sew body base to shell inserting legs through the seam and sewing into place. Secure safety eyes onto either side of head. Stuff head lightly, then sew pink mouth to underside of head. Sew green jaw over pink mouth to create bottom jaw. Sew head onto end of shell.

FINISHED SIZE: approx 4in. (10cm) long

Hippo

Hippos spend most of their lives in the water—apart from feeding time, when they eat up to 132lbs of grass a night. Their eyes and nostrils are at the top of the head so they can stay almost submerged to protect themsleves from the hot African sun.

BODY AND HEAD
Using MC, ch6, join with ss to make a ring.
Round 1: *2sc into next st, sc into foll st; rep from * twice more. (9 sts)
Round 2: *2sc into next st, sc into each of foll 2 sts; rep from * twice more. (12 sts)
Round 3: *1sc into each of next 3 sts, 2sc into foll st; rep from * twice more. (15 sts)
Round 4: *1sc into each of next 2 sts, 2sc into foll st; rep from * four times more. (20 sts)
Round 5: *1sc into each of next 3 sts, 2sc into foll st; rep from * four times more. (25 sts)
Round 6: *1sc into each of next 4 sts, 2sc into foll st; rep from * four times more. (30 sts)
Round 7: *1sc into each of next 5 sts, 2sc into foll st; rep from * four times more. (35 sts)
Round 8: *1sc into each of next 6 sts, 2sc into foll st; rep from * four times more. (40 sts)
Rounds 9–14: Work without inc.
Round 15: *1sc into each of next 6 sts, sc2tog; rep from * four times more. (35 sts)
Round 16: Work without dec.
Round 17: *1sc into each of next 5 sts, sc2tog; rep from * four times more. (30 sts)
Round 18: Work without dec.
Round 19: *1sc into each of next 4 sts, sc2tog; rep from * four times more. (25 sts)

Round 20: Work without dec.
Round 21: *1sc into each of next 3 sts, sc2tog; rep from * four times more. (20 sts)
Fasten off.

TOP JAW

Rejoin MC yarn into a st on last round of body and head, and cont to work along the edge. Work in rows.
Rows 1–6: Sc into each of the foll 8 sts, 1tch. (8 sts)
Fasten off.
Rejoin MC yarn to the base corner of rectangle, without using tch, work sc around three sides of jaw for another 2 rows.
Fasten off.

BOTTOM JAW

With the Upper jaw to the right, skip 2 sts, rejoin MC yarn into the last round of the Body and head and cont to work along the edge. Work in rows.
Rows 1–6: Sc into each of the foll 8 sts, 1tch. (8 sts)
Rejoin MC yarn to the base corner of the rectangle, without using tch, work sc around three sides of jaw for another 2 rows.
Fasten off.

INSIDE MOUTH

Using CC, ch9 plus one tch.
Row 1: Sc into the 2nd ch from the hook, sc into each ch to the end. (8 sts)
Rows 2–12: Sc into each st, 1tch
Fasten off.

FEET (MAKE 4)

Using MC, ch6, join with ss to make a ring.
Rows 1–2: Work without inc.

FINISHING

Secure safety eyes then stuff head and body. Place the inside mouth inside the top and bottom jaw and sew to secure. Sew on feet, using the photograph on page 70 as a guide for position.

TAIL

Using MC insert the hook into the foundation ring of the body and ch5.
Fasten off.

EAR

Using MC insert hook into top of head ch3, ss into the next st.
Rep once more for second ear.
Fasten off.

FINISHED SIZE: approx 4in. (10cm) long

You will need...

- 50g DK/light worsted yarn in Gray (MC)
- 25g same in Pink (CC)
- E/4 (3.5mm) crochet hook
- Pair 5mm black safety eyes
- Stuffing

abbreviations:

ch chain; **dec** decrease; **foll** following; **inc** increase; **rep** repeat; **sc** single crochet; **sc2tog** insert hook in st and draw up a loop. Insert hook in next st and draw up another loop. Yarn over, draw through all three loops on hook; **ss** slip stitch; **st(s)** stitch(es); **tch** turning chain

Guinea pig

Despite their name, these animals don't actually come from Guinea—they are natives to South America. After they were discovered by travelers in the 16th century they were brought over to Europe and soon became popular household pets.

BODY AND HEAD

The body is made in two pieces.
Using MC, ch6, join with ss to make a ring.

Rounds 1–2: Sc into each st.

Round 3: *2sc into next st, sc into foll st; rep from * twice more. (9 sts)

Round 4: *2sc into next st, sc into each of foll 2 sts; rep from * twice more. (12 sts)

Round 5: *Sc into each of next 3 sts, 2sc into foll st; rep from * twice more. (15 sts)

Round 6: *Sc into each of next 2 sts, 2sc into foll st; rep from * four times more. (20 sts)

Round 7: *Sc into each of next 3 sts, 2sc into foll st; rep from * four times more. (25 sts)

Round 8: Work without inc.

Round 9: *Sc into each of next 4 sts, 2sc into foll st; rep from * four times more. (30 sts)

Round 10: Work without inc.

Round 11: *Sc into each of next 5 sts, 2sc into foll st; rep from * four times more. (35 sts)

Round 12: Work without inc.

Round 13: *Sc into each of next 6 sts, 2sc into foll st; rep from * four times more. (40 sts)

Round 14: Work without inc.

Round 15: *Sc into each of next 7 sts, 2sc into foll st; rep from * four times more. (45 sts)

Round 16: Work without inc.

Round 17: *Sc into each of next 8 sts, 2sc into foll st; rep from * four times more. (50 sts)

Round 18: Work without inc.

Round 19: *Sc into each of next 9 sts, 2sc into foll st; rep from * four times more. (55 sts)

Rounds 20–25: Work without inc.
Fasten off.

BODY BASE

Using MC, ch6, join with ss to make a ring.

Round 1: *2sc into next st, sc into foll; rep from * twice more. (9 sts)

Round 2: *2sc into next st, sc into each of foll 2 sts; rep from * twice more. (12 sts)

Round 3: *Sc into each of next 3 sts, 2sc into foll st; rep from * twice more. (15 sts)

Round 4: *Sc into each of next 2 sts, 2sc into foll st; rep from * four times more. (20 sts)

Round 5: *Sc into each of next 3 sts, 2sc into foll st; rep from * four times more. (25 sts)

Round 6: *Sc into each of next 4 sts, 2sc into foll st; rep from * four times more. (30 sts)

Round 7: *Sc into each of next 5 sts, 2sc into foll st; rep from * four times more. (35 sts)

Round 8: *Sc into each of next 6 sts, 2sc into foll st; rep from * four times more. (40 sts)

Round 9: *Sc into each of next 7 sts, 2sc into foll st; rep from * four times more. (45 sts)

Round 10: *Sc into each of next 8 sts, 2sc into foll st; rep from * four times more. (50 sts)

Round 11: *Sc into each of next 9 sts, 2sc into foll st; rep from * four times more. (55 sts)
Fasten off.

EARS (MAKE 2)

Using CC, ch6, join with ss to make a ring.

Round 1: *2sc into next st, sc into foll st; rep from * twice more. (9 sts)

Round 2: *2sc into next st, sc into each of foll 2 sts; rep from * twice more. (12 sts)
Fasten off.

You will need...

- 50g DK/light worsted fluffy yarn in graduated colors (MC)
- 25g same in Pink (CC)
- E/4 (3.5mm) crochet hook
- Stuffing
- Slicker brush
- Pair 7.5mm black safety eyes
- Safety nose

abbreviations:

ch chain; **foll** following; **inc** increase; **rep** repeat; **sc** single crochet; **ss** slip stitch; **st(s)** stitch(es)

FEET (MAKE 4)

Using CC, join yarn to base of body, ch6, ss in first st, *ch6, ss in first st, rep from * once more
Rep once for each foot.
Fasten off.

FINISHING

Brush all pieces thoroughly with the slicker brush. Secure safety eyes and sew nose onto head using the photograph, right, as a guide. Stuff body and sew onto base. Sew ears onto each side of head and feet onto body, using the photograph as a guide.

FINISHED SIZE: approx 5in. (12.5cm) long

Anteater

This guy loves his six-legged snacks, but sometimes swallows them too quickly and forgets to chew. He can feel them tickling his belly as they look for a way out.

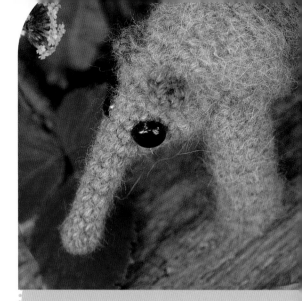

TAIL, BODY AND HEAD
Work in a continuous spiral.
Using MC, ch6, join with ss to make a ring.
Rounds 1–5: 1sc into each st.
Round 6: *2sc into next st, 1sc into foll st; rep from * twice more. (9 sts)
Round 7: Work without inc.
Round 8: *2sc into first st, sc into next 3 sts; rep twice more. (12 sts)
Round 9: Work without inc.
Round 10: *1sc into next 3 sts, 2sc into foll st; rep from * twice more. (15 sts)
Round 11: *1sc into next 2 sts, 2sc into foll st; rep from * four times more. (20 sts)
Round 12: *1sc into next 3 sts, 2sc into foll st; rep from * four times more. (25 sts)
Rounds 13–33: 1sc into each st.
Change to CC.
Rounds 34–45: 1sc into each st.
Round 46: *Sc2tog, 2sc into foll st; rep from * four times more. (20 sts)
Round 47: *Sc2tog, 2sc into foll st; from * four times more. (15 sts)
Stuff body.
Round 48: *Sc2tog, 3sc into next st; rep from * twice more. (12 sts)
Round 49: *Sc2tog to end. (6 sts)
Rounds 50–55: 1sc into each st.
Finish stuffing body and tail.
Fasten off.

LEGS (MAKE 4)
Using CC, ch10, join with ss to make a ring.
Rounds 1–10: 1sc into each st.
Fasten off.

FINISHING
Stuff legs and sew onto body, using the photograph on page 74 as a guide for positioning. Sew bead eyes or safety eyes onto head. Using CC, ch4 and secure in a loop on top of head to one side as one ear, rep on other side for other ear.

FINISHED SIZE: approx 10in. (25cm) long

You will need...

- 25g DK/light worsted yarn in Dark Brown (MC)
- 20g same in Light Brown (CC)
- E/4 (3.5mm) crochet hook
- Stuffing
- 2 small black beads, or pair of safety eyes
- Yarn needle

abbreviations:
ch chain; **foll** following **inc** increase; **rep** repeat; **sc** single crochet; **sc2tog** insert hook in st and draw up a loop. Insert hook in next st and draw up another loop. Yarn over, draw through all three loops on hook; **ss** slip stitch; **st(s)** stitch(es)

Underground overground

Butterfly

A lepidopterist is somebody who studies butterflies, and anybody who saw this beautiful example would no doubt have to take some time to admire the wings that are bursting with pretty colors. You don't have to use the yarns we've suggested; choose your own color schemes to give your butterfly a unique appearance.

You will need...

- 10g DK/light worsted yarn in Green (MC)
- 10g same in Blue (A)
- 10g same in Pink (B)
- 5g same in Orange (C)
- E/4 (3.5mm) crochet hook
- Stuffing
- Pair of 5mm beads or safety eyes
- Yarn needle

abbreviations:

ch chain; dc double crochet; foll following; inc increase; rep repeat; sc single crochet; sc2tog insert hook in st and draw up a loop. Insert hook in next st and draw up another loop. Yarn over, draw through all three loops on hook; ss slip stitch; st(s) stitch(es); tr triple crochet

BODY

Using MC, ch6, join with ss to make a ring.

Round 1: Sc into each st. (6 sts)

Round 2: *2sc into next st, sc into foll st; rep from * twice more. (9 sts)

Rounds 3–27: Work without inc.

Round 28: *Sc2tog, 1sc into foll st; rep from * twice more. (6 sts)

Fasten off.

TOP WING (MAKE 2)

Using A, ch9, join with ss to make a ring.

Round 1: Ch4 (do not count as a st), 2tr into each st, complete the round with a ss into the top of the first st. (18 sts)

Join in yarn B.

Round 2: Ch4 (do not count as a st), 2tr into each st, complete the round with a ss into the top of the first st. (36 sts)

Fasten off yarn B. Using yarn A.

Round 3: Ch3 (do not count as a st), *2dc into next st, 1dc into foll st; rep from * 17 times more, complete the round with a ss into the top of the first st. (54 sts)

Fasten off yarn A, join in yarn C.

Round 4: Ch1 (do not count as a st), sc into each st. (54 sts)

Fasten off.

BOTTOM WING (MAKE 2)

Using A, ch6, join with ss to make a ring.

Round 1: Ch 3 (do not count as a st), 2dc into each st, complete the round with a ss into the top of the first st. (12 sts)

Join in yarn B.

Round 2: Ch3 (count as 1st), *2dc into each of next 2 sts, 1dc in foll st; rep from * three times more, complete the round with a ss into the top of the first st. (21 sts)

Fasten off yarn B. Using yarn A.

Round 3: Ch3 (count as 1st), *2dc into each of next 2 sts, 1dc in foll st; rep from * six times more. complete the round with a ss into the top of the first st. (36 sts)

Fasten off yarn A, join in yarn C.

Round 4: Ch3 (do not count as a st), *2dc into next st, 1dc in foll st; rep from * 17 times more. (54 sts)

Fasten off.

FINISHING

Stuff the butterfly body. Sew on beads or secure safety eyes. Sew one top and one bottom wing onto either side of body, using the photo on page 79 as a guide.

ANTENNAE (MAKE 2)

Rejoin MC to the side of the head, ch4, fasten off and cut the tail ½in. (6mm) from the last ch. Rep on the other side of the head for the second antenna.

FINISHED SIZE: approx 6in. (15cm) long

Bluebird

The Eastern Bluebird is easily identifiable in the wild because of its bright blue back and colorful breast. They can be seen swooping down to munch on insects and other bugs in backyards across the east of the United States, and remain a firm favorite with birdwatchers across the globe.

UPPER BODY
Work in a continuous spiral.
Using MC, ch6, join with a ss to make a ring.
Work 8sc into center of ring.
Round 1: *2sc into next st, 1sc into foll st; rep from * to end of round. (12 sts)
Round 2: *2sc into next st, 1sc into foll st; rep from * five times more. (18 sts)
Round 3: *2sc into next st, 1sc in foll st, rep from * eight times more. (27 sts)
Round 4: *2sc into next st, 1sc in foll 8 sts; rep from * twice more. (30 sts)
Round 5: 1sc into each st to end of round.
Round 6: *2 sc into next st, 1sc in foll 4 sts; rep from * five times more. (36 sts)
Round 7: *2sc into next st, 1sc in foll 11 sts; rep from * twice more. (39 sts)
Round 8: *Sc2tog, 1sc in foll 10 sts; rep from * twice more. (36 sts)
Round 9: 1sc into each st to end of round.
Fasten off.

HEAD
Work in a continuous spiral.
Using MC, ch6, join with a ss to make a ring.
Work 8sc into center of ring.
Round 1: *2sc into next st, 1sc into foll st; rep from * to end of round. (12 sts)
Round 2: Work as round 1. (18 sts)
Round 3: Work as round 1. (27 sts)
Rounds 4–8: Work sc throughout.
Fasten off.

BODY
Work in a continuous spiral.
Using B, make a yarn ring, work 6sc into the ring.
Round 1: 2sc in each st to end of round. (12 sts)
Round 2: *1sc into next 3 sts, 2sc into foll st; rep from * twice more. (15 sts)
Round 3: *1sc into next 2 sts, 2sc into foll st; rep from * four times more. (20 sts)
Round 4: *1sc into next 3 sts, 2sc into foll st; rep from * four times more. (25 sts)
Round 5: *1sc into next 4 sts, 2sc into foll st; rep from * four times more. (30 sts)
Round 6: *1sc into next 5 sts, 2sc into foll st; rep from * four times more. (35 sts)
Round 7: *1sc into next 6 sts, 2sc into foll st; rep from * four times more. (40 sts)
Round 8: *1sc into next 7 sts, 2sc into foll st; rep from * four times more. (45 sts)
Rounds 9–12: Work in sc throughout.
Fasten off.

WINGS (MAKE 2)
Using MC, ch6, join with ss to make a ring.
Row 1: 4ch (counts as tr), 9tr into center of ring, turn.
Row 2: 3ch (counts as dc), 1dc into st at base of 3-ch, 2dc into each foll st to end of round. (20 sts).
Fasten off.

You will need...

- 15g of DK/light worsted yarn in Blue (MC)
- 15g same in Pink (B)
- Small amount of orange yarn for the beak (C)
- E/4 (3.5mm) crochet hook
- Pair of 7.5mm safety eyes or two small black beads
- Stuffing
- Yarn needle

abbreviations:
ch chain; **foll** following; **inc** increase; **rep** repeat; **sc** single crochet; **sc2tog** insert hook in st and draw up a loop. Insert hook in next st and draw up another loop. Yarn over, draw through all three loops on hook; **ss** slip stitch; **st(s)** stitch(es); **tch** turning chain; **tr** triple crochet

TAIL

Using MC, ch6.

Row 1: 1sc into each ch to end, 1tch, turn. (5 sts)

Row 2: 1sc into st at base of tch, 1dc into foll 3 sts, 2dc into final st, 1tch, turn. (7 sts)

Row 3: Work sc throughout, 1tch, turn.

Row 4: Work sc throughout, 1tch, turn.

Row 5: 3ch (counts as dc), work 1dc into st at base of 3-ch, 2dc into foll st, 1dc into foll 2 sts, 2dc into next 2 sts.

Fasten off.

FINISHING

Stuff lower body and sew to upper body.

Secure safety eyes or sew bead eyes onto head.

Stuff head and sew in place on upper body. Sew wings onto body either side of the head with wrong side facing. Sew tail in place at back of the upper body.

BEAK

Using C, ch4.

Fasten off.

Sew in place between the eyes to form a beak.

FINISHED SIZE: approx 3½in. (9cm) long

Toucan

Toucans love fruit; it's their main source of food, and they use their large beaks—which can sometimes be up to half the length of the body—to reach tasty treats hanging from branches. Different species have different-colored beaks so experiment with a variety of colored yarns for your crocheted version.

BEAK AND HEAD
Using A, ch2, join with ss to make a ring. Work 4sc into center of ring.

Rounds 1–2: Work in sc throughout. (4 sts)

Round 3: *2sc into next st, 1sc into foll st; rep from * once more. (6 sts)

Round 4: *2sc into next st, 1sc into foll 2sts; rep from * once more. (8 sts)
Change to B.

Rounds 5–8: Work in sc throughout. (8 sts)
Change to C.

Rounds 9–12: Work in sc throughout. (8 sts)
Divide for head.

NECK
Using CC, 1sc into next 4 sts, 1tch, turn. (4 sts)

Next row: 2sc into next st, 1sc into foll 2 sts, 2sc into foll st, 1tch, turn. (6 sts)
Work a further 6 rows as set.
Fasten off.

BACK OF HEAD
Using MC, rejoin yarn to first st to left side of CC stitch at top of beak, 1sc into next 4 sts, 1tch, turn. (4 sts)

Next row:
2sc into next st, 1sc into foll 2 sts, 2sc into foll st, 1tch, turn. (6 sts)
Work a further 6 rows as set.
Work 6 sc along top edge of neck piece, then a further 6 along top of back head. (12 sts)
Work one more round.
Fasten off.

BODY

Work in a continuous spiral.
Using B, make a yarn ring, work 6sc into the ring.
Round 1: *2sc into each st. (12 sts)
Round 2: *1sc into next 3 sts, 2sc into foll st; rep from * twice more. (15 sts)
Round 3: *1sc into next 2 sts, 2sc into foll st; rep from * four times more. (20 sts)
Round 4: *1sc into next 3 sts, 2sc into foll st; rep from * four times more. (25 sts)
Round 5: *1sc into next 4 sts, 2sc into foll st; rep from * four times more. (30 sts)
Round 6: *1sc into next 5 sts, 2sc into foll st; rep from * four times more. (35 sts)
Rounds 7–14: Work in sc throughout. (35 sts)
Round 15: *1sc into next 5 sts, sc2tog; rep from * to end of round. (30 sts)
Round 16: *1sc into next 4 sts, sc2tog; rep from * to end of round. (25 sts)
Round 17: *1sc into next 3 sts, sc2tog; rep from * to end of round. (20 sts)
Round 18: *1sc into next 2 sts, sc2tog; rep from * to end of round. (15 sts)
Round 19: *1sc into next st, sc2tog; rep from * to end of round. (10 sts)
Round 20: *1sc into next 3 sts, sc2tog; rep from * once more. (8 sts)
Rounds 21–22: Work in sc throughout. (8 sts)
Fasten off.

WINGS (MAKE 2)

Using MC, ch7.
Row 1: 1sc into each st. (6 sts)
Rows 2–4: 1sc into each st, 1tch, turn. (6 sts)
Rows 5–9: Work without tch to dec by one st on each row. (1 st)
Fasten off.

TAIL

Work in a continuous spiral.
Using MC, ch6, join with ss to make a ring.
Work 6sc into ring.
Round 1: 2sc into each st to end of round. (12 sts)
Round 2: Work in sc throughout. (12 sts)
Round 3: *1sc into next 3 sts, 2sc into foll st; rep from * to end of round. (15 sts)
Round 4: Work in sc throughout. (15 sts)
Round 5: *1sc into next 2 sts, 2sc into foll st; rep from * to end of round. (20 sts)
Rounds 6–10: Work in sc throughout. (20 sts)
Fasten off.
Sew a straight seam along final row to make a triangular shape.

FINISHING

Stuff body. Insert pipe cleaner through beak and stuff. Sew neck piece to back head, then stuff head. Sew head to body.
Brush body, head, tail, and wing pieces thoroughly. Sew wings and tail in place. Sew bead eyes on either side of head.

FINISHED SIZE: approx 5in. (12.5cm) high

You will need...

- Scraps of bright yarn in green (A), blue (B) and pink (C)
- 20g DK/light worsted fluffy yarn in Black (MC)
- 10g same in Yellow (CC)
- E/4 (3.5mm) crochet hook
- Stuffing
- Slicker brush
- Pair of black beads
- Pipe cleaner
- Yarn needle

abbreviations:

ch chain; foll following; inc increase; rep repeat; sc single crochet; sc2tog insert hook in st and draw up a loop. Insert hook in next st and draw up another loop. Yarn over, draw through all three loops on hook; ss slip stitch; st(s) stitch(es); tch turning chain

Owls

Owls are birds of the world, and you will find a species of them from Malaysia to Mexico. They are excellent hunters and benefit from special wings with serrated edges, which allow them to fly almost silently to capture prey. These cute versions love to sneak up and surprise people who are walking by.

You will need...

- 20g DK/light worsted self-striping yarn in Gray/Brown
- E/4 (3.5mm) crochet hook
- Stuffing
- Pair 15mm black safety eyes
- Small amount of pink yarn for embroidery
- Yarn needle

abbreviations:

ch chain; foll following; inc increase; rep repeat; sc single crochet; ss slip stitch; st(s) stitch(es)

BODY AND HEAD
Using MC, ch6, join with ss to make a ring.
Round 1: *2sc into next st, sc into foll st; rep from * twice more. (9 sts)
Round 2: *2sc into next st, sc into foll 2 sts; rep from * twice more. (12 sts)
Round 3: *Sc into each of next 3 sts, 2sc into foll st; rep from * twice more. (15 sts)
Round 4: *Sc into each of next 2 sts, 2sc into foll st; rep from * four times more. (20 sts)
Round 5: *Sc into each of next 3 sts, 2sc into foll st; rep from * four times more. (25 sts)
Rounds 6–14: Work without inc.
Fasten off.

FINISHING
Secure safety eyes to head, using the photograph on page 87 as a guide. Embroider beak. Stuff body and sew top gap together to make ears.

FINISHED SIZE: approx 3in. (7.5cm) high

Panda

There can't be many animals that are as adorable as pandas. There's something about their thick black and white fur that just makes you want to give them a hug. The reason for their coloring is not known, but their woolly coat keeps them warm in the cool Chinese forests that are their home.

You will need...

- 50g DK/light worsted fluffy yarn (such as Sirdar Blur) in White (MC)
- 25g same in Black (CC)
- E/4 (3.5mm) crochet hook
- Stuffing
- Slicker brush
- Pair 7.5mm black safety eyes
- Nose
- Yarn needle

abbreviations:

ch chain; **foll** following; **inc** increase; **rep** repeat; **sc** single crochet; **sc2tog** insert hook in st and draw up a loop. Insert hook in next st and draw up another loop. Yarn over, draw through all three loops on hook; **ss** slip stitch; **st(s)** stitch(es)

HEAD AND BODY

The body is made in two pieces starting at head end.

Work in a continuous spiral.

Using MC, ch6, join with ss to make a ring. Work 6sc into ring.

Rounds 1–2: Work without inc.

Round 3: *1sc into next st, 2sc into foll st; rep from * twice more. (9 sts)

Round 4: *1sc into next 3 sts, 2sc into foll st; rep from * twice more. (12 sts)

Round 5: *1sc into next 3 sts, 2sc into foll st; rep from * twice more. (15 sts)

Round 6: *1sc into next 2 sts, 2sc into foll st; rep from * four times more. (20 sts)

Round 7: *1sc into next 3 sts, 2sc into foll st; rep from * four times more. (25 sts)

Round 8: Work without inc.

Round 9: *1sc into next 4 sts, 2sc into foll st; rep from * four times more. (30 sts)

Rounds 10, 12, 14, 16, 18, 20, 22, 24: Work without inc.

Round 11: *1sc into next 5 sts, 2sc into foll st; rep from * four times more. (35 sts)

Round 13: *1sc into next 6 sts, 2sc into foll st; rep from * four times more. (40 sts)

Round 15: *1sc into next 7 sts, 2sc into foll st; rep from * four times more. (45 sts)

Round 17: *1sc into next 8 sts, 2sc into foll st; rep from * four times more. (50 sts)

Round 19: *1sc into next 9 sts, 2sc into foll st; rep from * four times more. (55 sts)

Round 21: *1sc into next 10 sts, 2sc into foll st; rep from * four times more. (60 sts)

Round 23: *1sc into next 11 sts, 2sc into foll st; rep from * four times more. (65 sts)

Round 25: *1sc into next 12 sts, 2sc into foll st; rep from * four times more. (70 sts)

Rounds 26–45: Work without inc.

Fasten off.

BODY BASE

Work in a continuous spiral. Using MC, ch6, join with ss to make a ring, work 6sc into ring.

Rounds 1–2: Work without inc.

Round 3: *1sc into next st, 2sc into foll st; rep from * twice more. (9 sts)

Round 4: *1sc into next 3 sts, 2sc into foll st; rep from * twice more. (12 sts)

Round 5: *1sc into next 3 sts, 2sc into foll st; rep from * twice more. (15 sts)

Round 6: *1sc into next 2 sts, 2sc into foll st; rep from * four times more. (20 sts)

Round 7: *1sc into next 3 sts, 2sc into foll st; rep from * four times more. (25 sts)

Round 8: Work without inc.

Round 9: *1sc into next 4 sts, 2sc into foll st; rep from * four times more. (30 sts)

Round 10: *1sc into next 5 sts, 2sc into foll st; rep from * four times more. (35 sts)

Round 11: *1sc into next 6 sts, 2sc into foll st; rep from * four times more. (40 sts)

Round 12: *1sc into next 7 sts, 2sc into foll st; rep from * four times more. (45 sts)

Round 13: *1sc into next 8 sts, 2sc into foll st; rep from * four times more. (50 sts)

Round 14: *1sc into next 9 sts, 2sc into foll st; rep from * four times more. (55 sts)

Round 15: *1sc into next 10 sts, 2sc into foll st; rep from * four times more. (60 sts)

Round 16: *1sc into next 11 sts, 2sc into foll st; rep from * four times more. (65 sts)

Round 17: *1sc into next 12 sts, 2sc into foll st; rep from * four times more. (70 sts)

Fasten off.

FACE PATCHES (MAKE 2)

Work in a continuous spiral.

Using CC, ch6, work 6sc into the ring.

Rounds 1–2: Work without inc.

Round 3: 2sc into each st to end twice more. (12 sts)

Round 4: *2sc into next st, 1sc into foll st; rep from * five times more. (18 sts)

Round 5: *2sc into next st, 1sc into foll 2 sts; rep from * five times more. (24 sts)

Fasten off.

LEGS (MAKE 2)

Work in a continuous spiral.

Using CC, ch6, work 6sc into the ring.

Rounds 1–2: Work without inc.

Round 3: *1sc into next st, 2sc into foll st; rep from * twice more. (9 sts)

Round 4: *1sc into next 3 sts, 2sc into foll st; rep from * twice more. (12 sts)

Round 5: *1sc into next 3 sts, 2sc into foll st; rep from * five times more. (15 sts)

Round 6: *1sc into next 2 sts, 2sc into foll st; rep from * five times more. (20 sts)

Round 7: *1sc into next 3 sts, 2sc into foll st; rep from * five times more. (25 sts)

Round 8: *1sc into next 4 sts, 2sc into foll st; rep from * five times more. (30 sts)

Rounds 9–30: Work without inc.

Round 31: *1sc into next 4 sts, sc2tog; rep from * five times more. (25 sts)

Round 32: *1sc into next 3 sts, sc2tog; rep from * five times more. (20 sts)

Round 33: *1sc into next 2 sts, sc2tog; rep from * five times more. (15 sts)

Round 34: *1sc into next 3 sts, sc2tog; rep from * twice more. (12 sts)

Round 35: Sc2tog in each st to end of round. (6 sts)

Fasten off.

ARMS (MAKE 2)

Work in a continuous spiral.

Using CC, ch6, work 6sc into the ring.

Rounds 1–2: Work without inc.

Round 3: *1sc into next st, 2sc into foll st, rep from * twice more. (9 sts)

Round 4: *1sc into next 3 sts, 2sc into foll st, rep from * twice more. (12 sts)

Round 5: *1sc into next 3 sts, 2sc into foll st; rep from * twice more. (15 sts)

Round 6: *1sc into next 2 sts, 2sc into foll st; rep from * four times more. (20 sts)

Round 7: *1sc into next 3 sts, 2sc into foll st; rep from * four times more. (25 sts)

Rounds 8–30: Work without inc.

Round 31: *1sc into next 3 sts, sc2tog; rep from * four times more. (20 sts)

Round 32: *1sc into next 2 sts, sc2tog; rep from * four times more. (15 sts)

Round 33: *1sc into next 3 sts, sc2tog; rep from * twice more. (12 sts)

Round 34: Sc2tog in each st to end of round. (6 sts)

Fasten off.

EARS (MAKE 2)

Work in a continuous spiral.

Make a yarn ring, work 6sc into the ring.

Round 1: *1sc into next st, 2sc into foll st; rep from * twice more. (9 sts)

Round 2: *1sc into next 3 sts, 2sc into foll st; rep from * twice more. (12 sts)

Round 3: *1sc into next 3 sts, 2sc into foll st; rep from * twice more. (15 sts)

Round 4: *1sc into next 2 sts, 2sc into foll st; rep from * four times more. (20 sts)

Round 5: *1sc into next 3 sts, 2sc into foll st; rep from * four times more. (25 sts)
Fasten off.

NOSE/MUZZLE
Work in a continuous spiral.
Make a yarn ring, work 8sc into the ring.
Round 1: *2sc into next st, 1sc into foll st; rep from * to end of round. (12 sts)
Round 2: Work as round 1. (18 sts)
Round 3: Work as round 1. (27 sts)
Rounds 4–6: Work without inc.
Fasten off.

FINISHING
Brush all pieces thoroughly with the slicker brush, paying particular attention to where eyes will be fitted, because if you have to brush here again later you can scratch the eyes. Secure nose to end of muzzle, stuff muzzle and sew onto head. Secure safety eyes to head through eye patches. Stuff body and sew on base. Stuff legs and sew to body using the photograph on page 89 as a guide. Embroider mouth.

FINISHED SIZE: approx 7½in. (19cm) long

tip:

To make the Panda sit up nicely, you could insert a bag of plastic pellets into the base of the body to weight it, before sewing the final seam.

Koala

Although often called bears and strongly resembling other members of the species, koalas are not linked to the bear family at all. This koala loves nothing more than a snooze in the midday sun and, like his relatives, will remain asleep for around 16 to 18 hours a day after a busy lunch spent munching on eucalyptus leaves.

BODY

Using MC, ch6, join with ss to make a ring.

Round 1: 2sc in each st. (12 sts)

Round 2: *1sc into next 3 sts, 2sc into foll st; rep from * twice more. (15 sts)

Round 3: *1sc into next 2 sts, 2sc into foll st; rep from * four times more. (20 sts)

Round 4: *1sc into next 3 sts, 2sc into foll st; rep from * four times more. (25 sts)

Round 5: *1sc into next 4 sts, 2sc into foll st; rep from * four times more. (30 sts)

Round 6: *1sc into next 5 sts, 2sc into foll st; rep from * four times more. (35 sts)

Rounds 7–15: Work without inc.

Round 16: *1sc into 5 sts, sc2tog; rep from * four times more. (30 sts)

Round 17: *1sc into 4 sts, sc2tog; rep from * four times more. (25 sts)

Round 18: *1sc into 3 sts, sc2tog; rep from * four times more. (20 sts)

Round 19: *1sc into 2 sts, sc2tog; rep from * four times more. (15 sts)

Place last st on a stitch holder.

Stuff body.

Place held st back onto crochet hook.

Round 20: *1sc into 3 sts, sc2tog; rep from * twice more. (12 sts)

Round 21: Sc2tog to end. (6 sts)

Fasten off.

HEAD (MAKE 2)

Using MC, ch6, join with ss to make a ring.

Round 1: 2sc in each st. (12 sts)

Round 2: *1sc into next 3 sts, 2sc into foll st; rep from * twice more. (15 sts)

Round 3: *1sc into next 2 sts, 2sc into foll st; rep from * four times more. (20 sts)

Round 4: *1sc into next 3 sts, 2sc into foll st; rep from * four times more. (25 sts)

Round 5: *1sc into next 4 sts, 2sc into foll st; rep from * four times more. (30 sts)

Round 6: *1sc into next 5 sts, 2sc into foll st; rep from * four times more. (35 sts)

Round 7: *1sc into next 6 sts, 2sc into foll st; rep from * four times more. (40 sts)

Round 8: *1sc into next 7 sts, 2sc into foll st; rep from * four times more. (45 sts)

Round 9: *1sc into next 6 sts, 2sc into foll st; rep from * four times more. (50 sts)

Fasten off.

LEGS (MAKE 4)

Work in a continuous spiral.

Make a yarn ring, work 8sc into the ring.

Rounds 1–7: Work in sc throughout without inc. (8 sts)

Fasten off.

EARS (MAKE 2)

Using MC, ch6, join with ss to make a ring.

Round 1: 2sc in each st to end. (12 sts)

Next row: 1sc into next 6 sts, 1tch, turn.

Next row: 2sc into next st, 1sc into each foll st to end of row, 1tch, turn. (7 sts)

Next row: 1sc into each st to end of row.

Next row: 2sc into next st, 1sc into each foll st to end of row. (8 sts)

Fasten off.

FINISHING

Brush ear pieces thoroughly with a slicker brush. Sew bead eyes or secure safety eyes onto one side of head. Sew two sides of head together, adding some stuffing before completing the seam. Attach ears and embroider nose, using the photograph on page 92 as a guide. Sew head onto body. Sew legs to body.

FINISHED SIZE: approx 4in. (10cm) high

You will need...

- 25g DK/light worsted yarn in Gray
- E/4 (3.5mm) crochet hook
- Stitch holder
- 2 small black beads, or safety eyes
- Stuffing
- Slicker brush
- Small amount of brown yarn for embroidery
- Yarn needle

abbreviations:

ch chain; **foll** following; **inc** increase; **rep** repeat; **sc** single crochet; **sc2tog** insert hook in st and draw up a loop. Insert hook in next st and draw up another loop. Yarn over, draw through all three loops on hook; **ss** slip stitch; **st(s)** stitch(es)

Silkworm

A single silkworm can produce a thread of silk up to 3,000 feet long—taller than two Empire State Buildings stacked on top of each other. Unfortunately silk is not that easy to use for crocheting, but colorful worsted yarn works just as well.

You will need...

- 25g DK/light worsted yarn in Green (MC)
- 20g same in Orange (CC)
- E/4 (3.5mm) crochet hook
- Pair of large safety eyes or beads
- Stuffing
- Pipe cleaner
- Yarn needle

abbreviations:

ch chain; foll following; inc increase; rep repeat; sc single crochet; sc2tog insert hook in st and draw up a loop. Insert hook in next st and draw up another loop. Yarn over, draw through all three loops on hook; ss slip stitch; st(s) stitch(es)

HEAD

Work in a continuous spiral.
Using MC, make a yarn ring, work 6sc into the ring.
Round 1: 2sc in each st to end of round. (12 sts)
Round 2: *1sc into next 3 sts, 2sc into foll st; rep from * twice more. (15 sts)
Round 3: *1sc into next 2 sts, 2sc into foll st; rep from * four times more. (20 sts)
Round 4: *1sc into next 3 sts, 2sc into foll st; rep from * four times more. (25 sts)
Round 5: *1sc into next 4 sts, 2sc into foll st; rep from * four times more. (30 sts)
From this point the Caterpillar is worked in two pieces.

TOP SIDE

Place marker into last st.
Work 1sc into next 10 sts. Place marker into next st on previous row, 1tch, turn.
Working on these 10 sts only, work in sc throughout until 50 rows are completed from marker.
Fasten off.

UNDERSIDE

Insert hook into marked st to left side of top side.
Work 1sc into next 20 sts, 1tch, turn.
Working on these 20 sts only, work in sc throughout until 50 rows are completed from marker.

Fasten off.
From this point the Caterpillar is worked in one piece.
To join the pieces, with right side facing, work a row of sc along the side edge of the top side and under side seams simultaneously, 1tch, turn.
Work one row sc.
Fasten off, leaving one seam open.

TAIL

Round 1: Insert hook into first st to the side of a seam. Work 1sc into each st to end of round. (30 sts)
Round 2: *1sc into next 4 sts, sc2tog; rep from * four times more. (25 sts)
Rounds 3, 5, 7: Work in sc to end of round.
Round 4: *1sc into next 3 sts, sc2tog; rep from * four times more. (20 sts)
Round 6: *1sc into next 2 sts, sc2tog; rep from * four times more. (15 sts)
Round 8: *1sc into next 3 sts, sc2tog; rep from * twice more. (12 sts)
Round 9: Sc2tog to end of round. (6 sts)
Fasten off.

FINISHING

Sew bead eyes or secure safety eyes onto head. Insert pipe cleaner into body and stuff. With right side facing, work a row of sc along side edge of top side and under side seams simultaneously, 1tch, turn.
Work one row sc.
Fasten off.

FEELERS (MAKE 2)
Using CC, ch8.
Fasten off.
Sew to ridges made by seams above eyes.

BACK RIDGE
Insert hook into center point of top side, *ch10,
1sc into foll 2 sts in line with last st; rep from *
until 28 loops completed.
Fasten off.

FINISHED SIZE: approx 10in. (25cm) long

Star-nosed mole

Star-nosed moles are pretty unusual looking creatures. They get their name from the ultra-sensitive tentacles at the end of their face, which they use to help them locate and consume food. They live close to streams or ponds and are excellent swimmers, with their tunnels often exiting into water so they can make a quick exit and search for something tasty to eat.

BODY
Work in a continuous spiral.
Using MC, ch6, join with ss to make a ring.
Work 6sc into ring.
Round 1: 2sc into each st to end of round. (12 sts)
Round 2: *1sc into next 3 sts, 2sc into foll st; rep from * twice more. (15 sts)
Round 3: *1sc into next 2 sts, 2sc into foll st; rep from * four times more. (20 sts)
Round 4: *1sc into next 3 sts, 2sc into foll st; rep from * four times more. (25 sts)
Round 5: *1sc into next 4 sts, 2sc into foll st; rep from * four times more. (30 sts)
Round 6: *1sc into next 5 sts, 2sc into foll st; rep from * four times more. (35 sts)
Round 7: *1sc into next 6 sts, 2sc into foll st; rep from * four times more. (40 sts)
Round 8: *1sc into next 7 sts, 2sc into foll st; rep from * four times more. (45 sts)
Rounds 9–20: Work without inc.
Fasten off.

NOSE
Using CC, cut 20 lengths of yarn approx 5in. (12cm) long. Holding the lengths as a bunch, tie a knot at the center point. Insert the crochet hook through the ring created at the beginning of the body and draw cut yarn ends through. Trim.

FEET (MAKE 4)
Using CC, *ch10, join with ss into first chain; rep from * twice more.
Fasten off.

FINISHING
Brush body thoroughly with a slicker brush. Secure safety eyes to head. Stuff body. Sew a straight seam along the final row to make a triangular shape. Sew two of the feet in place at corners. Sew remaining feet in place halfway up body.

FINISHED SIZE: approx 4in. (10cm) long

You will need...
- 25g DK/light worsted fluffy yarn (such as Sirdar Blur) in Dark Brown (MC)
- 5g same in Pink (CC)
- E/4 (3.5mm) crochet hook
- 2 small black beads, or safety eyes
- Slicker brush
- Stuffing
- Yarn needle

abbreviations:
ch chain; foll following; inc increase; rep repeat; sc single crochet; ss slip stitch; st(s) stitch(es)

Arctic fox

Arctic foxes live in some of the coldest conditions on the planet, in frozen areas in Russia, northern Scandinavia, and Canada. They need a thick coat of fur to keep them warm while walking on the snow and ice. This project lends itself well to the brush crochet technique, because this emphasizes the depth of the fox's coat.

You will need...

- 25g DK/light worsted fluffy yarn in White (MC)
- 10g same in Beige (CC)
- E/4 (3.5mm) crochet hook
- Stuffing
- Slicker brush
- Pair 20mm black safety eyes
- Pipe cleaners
- Black embroidery thread for nose
- Brown sewing thread for mouth
- Yarn needle

abbreviations:

ch chain; foll following; inc increase; rep repeat; sc single crochet; sc2tog insert hook in st and draw up a loop. Insert hook in next st and draw up another loop. Yarn over, draw through all three loops on hook; ss slip stitch; st(s) stitch(es); tch turning chain

BODY
Using MC, ch6, join with ss to make a ring.
Round 1: *2sc into next st, 1sc into foll st; rep from * twice more. (9 sts)
Round 2: *2sc into next st, 1sc into foll 2 sts; rep from * twice more. (12 sts)
Round 3: *1sc into next 3 sts, 2sc into foll st; rep from * twice more. (15 sts)
Round 4: *1sc into next 2 sts, 2sc into foll st; rep from * four times more. (20 sts)
Round 5: *1sc into next 3 sts, 2sc into foll st; rep from * four times more. (25 sts)
Rounds 6–10: Work without inc.
Round 11: *1sc into next 3 sts, sc2tog; rep from * four times more. (20 sts)
Round 12: *1sc into next 2 sts, sc2tog; rep from * four times more. (15 sts)
Stuff body.
Round 13: *1sc into next 3 sts, sc2tog; rep from * twice more. (12 sts)
Round 14: *Sc2tog, 1sc into foll 2 sts; rep from * twice more. (9 sts)
Round 15: *Sc2tog, 1sc into st; rep from * twice more. (6 sts)
Fasten off.

HEAD (MAKE 2)
Using MC, ch6, join with ss to make a ring.
Round 1: *2sc into next st, 1sc into foll st; rep from * twice more. (9 sts)
Round 2: *2sc into next st, 1sc into foll 2 sts; rep from * twice more. (12 sts)
Round 3: *1sc into next 3 sts, 2sc into foll st; rep from * twice more. (15 sts)
Round 4: *1sc into next 2 sts, 2sc into foll st; rep from * four times more. (20 sts)
Round 5: *1sc into next 3 sts, 2sc into foll st; rep from * four times more. (25 sts)
Round 6: *1sc into next 4 sts, 2sc into foll st; rep from * four times more. (30 sts)
Round 7: *1sc into next 5 sts, 2sc into foll st; rep from * four times more. (35 sts)
Round 8: *1sc into next 6 sts, 2sc into foll st; rep from * four times more. (40 sts)
Fasten off.

SNOUT
Using MC, ch6, join with ss to make a ring.
Round 1: *2sc into next st, 1sc into foll st; rep from * twice more. (9 sts)
Round 2: *2sc into next st, 1sc into foll 2 sts; rep from * twice more. (12 sts)
Round 3: *1sc into next 3 sts, 2sc into foll st; rep from * twice more. (15 sts)
Fasten off.

LEGS (MAKE 4)
Using MC, ch6, join with ss to make a ring.
Round 1: *2sc into next st, 1sc into foll st; rep from * twice more. (9 sts)
Rounds 2–20: Work without inc.
Fasten off.

EARS
Rejoin CC, ch8 into one side of head then decrease naturally on each row by not using a tch.
Work one row of sc around each ear.
Fasten off.

TAIL
Using CC, ch6, join with ss to make a ring.
Round 1: *2sc into next st, 1sc into foll st; rep from * twice more. (9 sts)
Round 2: *2sc into first st, 1sc into foll 2 sts; rep from * twice more. (12 sts)
Rounds 3–20: Work without inc.
Fasten off.

FINISHING
Brush all pieces thoroughly with the slicker brush. Secure safety eyes and stitch snout to one of the head pieces. Sew the two head pieces together then stuff the head. Sew the head to the body. Sew the tail to the rear of the body. Stuff each leg with a length of pipe cleaner, sew legs to body and arrange in an attractive position.

FINISHED SIZE: approx 5in. (12.5cm) high

Dragon

Dragons feature in the myths and legends of countries across the globe. In Europe they tend to be winged, fire breathing monsters that cause damage to humans, while in China they are a symbol of good luck and strength. This little version is based on the Chinese friendlier type, but the colors have been inspired by the national symbol of Wales, Y Ddraig Goch. According to legend, this red dragon defeated a marauding white dragon, saving the subjects of King Vortigern in the process.

You will need...

- 20g DK/light worsted yarn in Red (MC)
- 10g same in Green (CC)
- E/4 (3.5mm) crochet hook
- Stuffing
- Pair of 8mm black safety eyes

abbreviations:

ch chain; **dec** decrease; **foll** following; **inc** increase; **rep** repeat; **sc** single crochet; **sc2tog** insert hook in st and draw up a loop. Insert hook in next st and draw up another loop. Yarn over, draw through all three loops on hook; **ss** slip stitch; **st(s)** stitch(es)

BODY

Using MC, ch6, join with ss to make a ring.

Round 1: 2sc into each st. (12 sts)

Round 2: *2sc into next st, sc into foll st; rep from * five more times. (18 sts)

Round 3: *2sc into next st, sc into each of foll 2 sts; rep from * five more times. (24 sts)

Round 4: *2sc into next st, sc into each of foll 3 sts; rep from * five more times. (30 sts)

Rounds 5–10: Work without inc.

Stuff body.

Round 11: *Sc2tog, sc into each of foll 3 sts; rep from * five more times. (24 sts)

Round 12: *Sc2tog, sc into each of foll 2 sts; rep from * five more times. (18 sts)

Round 13: *Sc2tog, sc into foll st; rep from * five more times. (12 sts)

Rounds 14–20: Work without dec.

Stuff body.

Round 21: Sc2tog six times. (6 sts)

Fasten off.

HEAD

Using MC, ch6, join with ss to make a ring.

Round 1: 2sc into each st. (12 sts)

Round 2: *2sc into next st, sc into foll st; rep from * five more times. (18 sts)

Round 3: *2sc into next st, sc into each of foll 2 sts; rep from * five more times. (24 sts)

Round 4: *2sc into next st, sc into each of foll 3 sts; rep from * five more times. (30 sts)

Rounds 5–10: Work without inc.

Fasten off.

NOSE

Using MC, ch6, join with ss to make a ring.

Round 1: Sc into each st. (6 sts)

Round 2: 2sc into each st. (12 sts)

Rounds 3–4: Work without inc.

Fasten off.

FINISHING

Secure safety eyes. Stuff head and sew top gap together to make ears Sew nose onto head and head onto body.

FEET (MAKE 2)

Using CC, *ch8, ss into first st, rep from twice more.
Rep once more for other foot.
Fasten off.
Sew on feet.

BACK SPINES

Using CC, join yarn to the back of the head between the ears, then, crocheting into the body along the back, *ch10 then crochet back into body to create a spiky ridge, rep from * to the tail.

FINISHED SIZE: approx 4in. (10cm) long

tips:

This little dragon has no legs—he sits on his little fat stomach and frilly feet. This makes him fast to make because you don't have to create extra pieces and sew them on. If you want to add legs, make a suitable set by following the instructions from one of the other patterns.

As an alternative to the chain loop ridge, you could work the ridge down the back in the same way as on the Crocodile, on page 40.

The simple rounded shape of this toy is ideal for tiny hands.

For a small child make sure you sew the head on very firmly, so there is no danger it can be pulled off by accident.

The red and green coloring used here are the national colors of Wales. For a Chinese dragon, try making him in yellow and turquoise, as if he were made of gold and enamel. Or you could use red and black, like the colors in a Chinese lacquer box.

Techniques

Here are all the techniques you will need to complete the projects in this book. Once you have got the hang of the basic stitches, you can create super-cute creatures in no time at all.

Making a slip knot

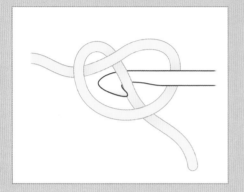 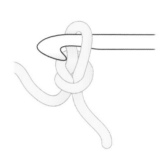 

1. Start by making a circle with the yarn. Put the hook through the loop and catch the tail of the yarn.

2. Form a loop by pulling the yarn then pull the knot gently to close the loop on the hook.

Holding the hook

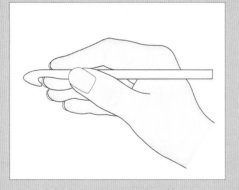

Hold the hook as if it was a pencil or a pen in between your index finger and thumb. Don't grip it too tightly, so that you can move it quickly and easily.

Holding the yarn

If you hold the hook in your right hand, with your palm facing upwards pick up the yarn with the little finger of your left hand and then turn it over. The yarn should now be under your ring and middle finger and on top of your index finger. Hold the work just below the slip knot between your index finger and thumb.

Yarn over hook

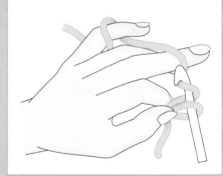

Pull the yarn through the loop by catching it from behind with the tip of the hook to make a stitch. Keep the loop loose so that the hook can pass through it easily.

Chain

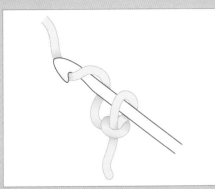 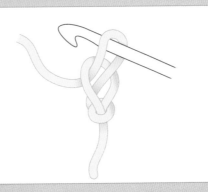

1. Following the instructions for yarn over hook, pull the yarn through the loop with the hook tip to make a new loop on the hook. Repeat the process again, pulling the yarn through the loop to create a chain of stitches.

2. Count the number of stitches as you go along until you have the amount required by the pattern. Hold the work in place between the middle finger and thumb of your left hand, just below the stitch you are working into.

Chain ring/circle

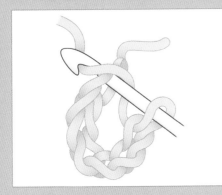 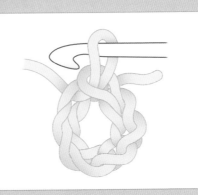

1. Once you have finished making a chain, you can make a ring by inserting the hook into the first chain and then yarn over hook.

2. Next, feed the yarn through the chain and the loop on the hook.

Marking rounds

When working in a continuous spiral it is essential you mark the beginning/end of the round. You can buy plastic stitch markers that just clip onto the yarn, but you can easily make your own marker by simply threading a short piece of contrast yarn through the work and knotting loosely.

Slip stich

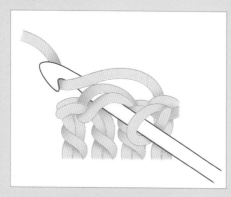

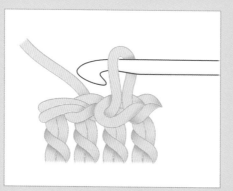

1. Slip stitches are short stitches that do not create any height. To make one, insert the hook into the stitch and catch the yarn.

2. Pull the yarn through the stitch and the loop on the hook.

Single crochet

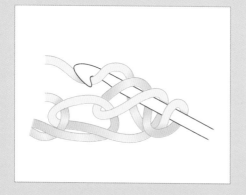

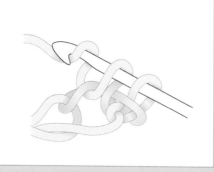

1. Insert the hook into the required stitch, yarn over hook as you do for slip stitch. Pull the yarn through just the stitch, not the loop as well, so you now have two loops on the hook.

2. Catch the yarn with the hook and pull it through both loops on the hook.

Half double crochet

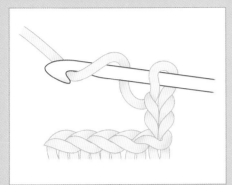

1. Wrap the yarn over the hook and put it through the work.

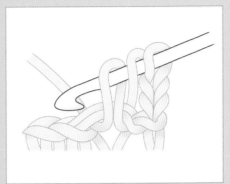

2. Yarn over the hook again and pull a new loop through to give you three loops on the hook.

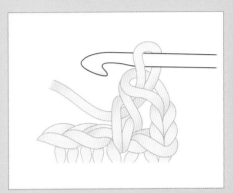

3. Pull a loop through all three loops to give you one loop on the hook.

Double crochet

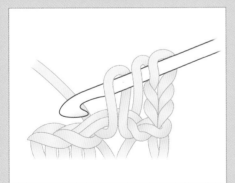

1. This is similar to the first two steps of the half double. Wrap your yarn over the hook and put it through the work.

2. Yarn over the hook and pull through a new loop to give you three loops on the hook. Wrap the yarn over the hook again and pull it through the first two loops.

3. Wrap the yarn over the hook again and pull it though the next two hooks to leave one loop on the hook.

Making rows

Use a turning chain at the end of a row to make a stitch that is high enough for the stitch you are working with. A single crochet stitch will require one chain, a half double crochet will require two chains, and double crochet requires three chains to match the height.

Joining new yarn

If you come to the end of the yarn when working in single crochet, you can attach a new yarn by inserting the hook into the stitch as normal and pulling through a loop with the original yarn. Next take the new yarn, wrap it over the hookn and pull it through the two loops to fix the two lengths together.

Brush crochet

I developed the brush crochet technique in order to make my furry amigurumi animals even more adorable. It is such a simple idea and can easily be applied for any animal that has fur, all you need is a slicker brush. I use a standard animal grooming brush, the kind you can pick up in any pet store. You need a slicker brush because an ordinary brush or comb won't do the job of fluffing the hair as effectively.

Rub the brush all over the toy, going backward and forward to get all the yarn fluffed up. Don't be afraid to really get stuck in, you have to be quite vigorous in order to get the desired effect. Very quickly you will start to see the threads of the yarn start to come loose and resemble fur.

Make sure you brush the animal before you attach its eyes, because the plastic can easily be damaged by the brush.

Decreasing

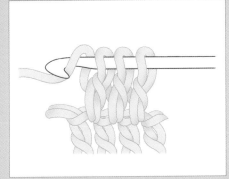

There are two ways to decrease. The first method is to single crochet two stitches together by inserting your hook into the required stitch, wrapping the yarn over the hook and pulling it though to give you two loops on the hook. Put the hook into the next stitch, wrap the yarn over the hook and again pull the yarn through the work to give you three loops on the hook. Finish by catching the yarn on the hook and pulling it through all three of the loops.

The second method is to simply miss the next stitch and carry on crocheting.

You can decease by either missing the next stitch and continue crocheting, or by single crocheting two stitches together (sc2tog) as follows: insert hook in st and draw up a loop. Insert hook in next st and draw up another loop. Yarn over, draw through all three loops on hook.

Increasing

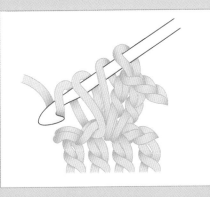

To increase, create two stitches in one stitch of the previous row.

Working into a ring of yarn

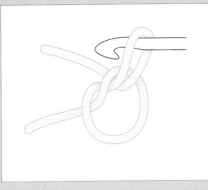

Rings of yarn can be drawn up tightly to make a neat, unobtrusive center. Always darn in the yarn end securely.

Wind the yarn once around the first finger of the left hand. Insert the hook in the ring, yarn over hook and pull through ring, yarn over hook and pull through to make the first chain. Work stitches into the ring, then pull the end to tighten the ring before joining the round.

Suppliers

YARN SUPPLIERS

Adriafil Yarns
www.adriafil.com for stockists

Anny Blatt
www.annyblatt.com for stockists

Debbie Bliss
www.debbieblissonline.com

Bouton D'or
www.boutondor.com

Coats Craft Rowan Yarns
www.coatscrafts.co.uk

Colinette Yarns
www.colinette.com for stockists

Gedifra
Available from www.yarnmarket.com

Knitglobal
www.knitglobal.com

Lana Grossa
www.lanagrossa.com for stockists

Lanartus Yarns
www.lanartus.net

Lang Yarns
www.langyarns.ch/en

Louisa Harding
www.louisaharding.co.uk

Noro Yarns
www.noroyarns.com
for stockists

Patons Yarns
www.patonsyarns.co.uk
Presencia
www.presenciausa.com
for stockists

RY Classic Yarns
www.ryclassic.com

Sirdar Yarns
www.sirdar.co.uk

South West Trading Company (SWTC) Yarns
www.soysilk.com

Stef Francis
www.stef-francis.co.uk

Trendsetter Yarns
www.trendsetteryarns.com

Twilleys of Stamford
www.twilleys.co.uk for stockists

Wensleydale Longwool
www.wensleydalelongwoolsheepshop.co.uk

STOCKISTS

A.C. Moore
Stores nationwide
1-888-226-6673
www.acmoore.com

Hobby Lobby
Stores nationwide
www.hobbylobby.com

Jo-Ann Fabric and Craft Store
Stores nationwide
1-888-739-4120
www.joann.com

Knitting Fever
Stockists of Debbie Bliss, Noro, and Sirdar yarns
www.knittingfever.com

Knitting Garden
Stockists of Rowan yarns
www.theknittinggarden.com

Lets Knit
www.letsknit.com

Michaels
Stores nationwide
1-800-642-4235
www.michaels.com

Unicorn Books and Crafts
www.unicornbooks.com

WEBS
www.yarn.com

Yarn Market
www.yarnmarket.com

BLOG

Roman Sock
littlegreen.typepad.com/romansock

Index

Acknowledgments

For Pauline—the greatest inspiration I could ever have.

I couldn't have done this without encouragement from June, Karen, Tayloure, and, of course, my wonderful Mum and Dad.

I am forever grateful to Pete and Cindy from CICO Books who have been fabulous, Luis for the design, and to Marie Clayton, Jane Crowfoot, and Luise Roberts for making sense of my scribblings.

A big thank you to JW, LC, AS, LR, SD, and AK for putting up with me, and my love of amigurumi.

Finally, in memory of Twinks who started it all.